BECOMING A
FULLY ALIGNED
STUDENT-CENTERED
ORGANIZATION

ADVANCE PRAISE

"Tired of putting out fires instead of leading? *Becoming a Fully Aligned Student-Centered Organization* gives school leaders the clarity, tools, and confidence to put students back at the center and build schools that thrive."

TREVOR MUIR
Educator. Author. Speaker.

"As a former district superintendent and now a leadership studies instructor working with aspiring building and district leaders, I see every day how overwhelming the demands of educational leadership can be. Kevin Stoller's *Becoming a Fully Aligned Student-Centered Organization* is a timely and valuable resource that cuts through the noise. The FASCO framework offers a practical structure that helps leaders shift from constantly reacting to leading with clarity and purpose."

DR. JOE FISHER
Retired Superintendent,
Arkansas Public Schools

"Most school leaders don't need another gimmick—they need a system. FASCO delivers. Built on six proven tools and grounded in student-centered principles, the Fully Aligned Student-Centered Organization model gives leaders a clear, step-by-step way to make better decisions, spend their time wisely, and lead with purpose. Drawing on the truth that 'every system is perfectly designed to get the results it gets,' FASCO helps you replace outdated, autopilot processes with a framework that actually works—for students, staff, and community! Learn it, live it, and leave a legacy of alignment that lasts long after you've moved on."

JETHRO JONES
Founder of Transformative Principal

"As an educational leader for over twenty years and a board member for ELO, I've seen firsthand the tension school leaders carry—not from apathy, but from a deep misalignment between intention and action. This book gives voice to that silent struggle. FASCO is more than a framework; it's a clarifying system that reconnects schools to what matters most—students. It's honest, practical, and long overdue."

DR. BRAD UCHACZ
Vice President, Imagine Schools
Board Member, ELO

"As an executive director, I found *Becoming a Fully Aligned Student-Centered Organization* to be both affirming and transformative. It captures the relentless pace, the competing priorities, and the personal sacrifices school leaders know all too well. It validates our challenges and offers a practical, sustainable framework to overcome them. The FASCO model provides a clear, step-by-step approach to aligning teams, clarifying priorities, and keeping students truly at the center of every decision. This is not another educational fad—it's a blueprint for creating focus, empowering leaders at all levels, and building systems that last. Any leader serious about improving outcomes for students while preserving their own capacity to lead should read this book."

DAN GIRARD
Executive Director of Elementary Education,
South-Western City Schools

"FASCO is the systems guide for school leaders that provides clear, actionable, and value-driven tools. This book provides a blueprint and student-centered structures for transforming education systems into resilient, agile, and aligned systems that are truly effective and mission-driven."

ELLEN PERCONTI
Superintendent, Goldendale School District

BECOMING A

FULLY

The Guide for School Leaders

ALIGNED

STUDENT

CENTERED

ORGANIZATION

KEVIN STOLLER

Executive Director, Education Leaders' Organization

BECOMING A FULLY ALIGNED
STUDENT-CENTERED ORGANIZATION
The Guide for School Leaders

Copyright © 2026 by Kevin Stoller

Disclaimer: This book has been published for the purpose of providing the reader with general information on its subject matter. The author and the publisher believe the information to be accurate and authoritative at the time of publication. The book is sold with the understanding that neither the author nor the publisher is providing professional advice, and the reader should not rely upon this book as such. Every situation is different, and professional advice (whether psychological, legal, financial, tax, or otherwise) should only be obtained from a professional licensed in your jurisdiction who has knowledge of the specific facts and circumstances.

Book Cover Design by Rachel Royer
Interior Layout and Design by Stephanie Anderson
Editorial Team: Traci Matt, Ginny Glass, Marcie Taylor, Rachel Maier

Isbns:
979-8-89165-362-7 *Paperback*
979-8-89165-363-4 *Hardback*
979-8-89165-361-0 *E-book*

Published by:
Streamline Books
Kansas City, MO
ShareYourStory.com

To the school leaders who have given their lives to helping students grow and succeed—those who spend their evenings planning, their weekends learning, and their "summers off" working, in order to support programs, facilities, staff, and families.

To those who show up early, stay late, and pour themselves into every extracurricular, every conversation, every crisis, and every quiet moment where a student just needs someone to care.

To the leaders who continue chasing a better way, even when the system makes it hard. Those who believe every child deserves a chance, and who keep believing—even on the days it feels impossible.

This book is for you.

Thank you for your commitment, your courage, and the impact you make that few truly see but generations will feel.

CONTENTS

FOREWORD

School leadership has become more challenging than ever. Districts and schools are pushed in many directions—new mandates, competing initiatives, accountability pressures, and daily struggles to keep classrooms and communities functioning well. Leaders understand the importance of their work, but many feel overwhelmed, constantly responding to crises instead of moving forward with clarity and purpose.

In my journey as a superintendent and later as the leader of a national nonprofit focused on future-ready learning, I experienced this tension firsthand. I sat with many teams where everyone cared deeply, but no one was certain who truly owned the work. I saw data dashboards grow, but meaning and focus lessened. I observed leaders stretched thin, eager to serve students but unsure how to align adults with what mattered most.

What was missing was not vision or will. What was missing was coherence.

That is why FASCO—the Fully Aligned Student-Centered Organization—matters. It offers the coherence leaders seek. Developed from real-world experience and tested by superintendents and district teams, FASCO provides something rare: a system that is both practical and transformative.

FASCO is built around a core set of tools that work together to create alignment and momentum. It starts with the Accountability Circle, which clarifies ownership, so every critical function has a clear, visible steward. Next, Vitals make progress measurable by assigning each role a number that indicates whether the system is healthy. Weekly Huddles establish a disciplined rhythm that prevents drift and fosters trust, while Rocks set the priorities for the next ninety days to keep teams focused on what matters most. Methods define the "how," ensuring the best work survives beyond any single leader or moment. Vision, placed intentionally at the end rather than the beginning, becomes more than just a slogan—it acts as a bold, actionable north star rooted in real structures. ACE coaching brings the system to life, combining challenge with support so that leadership remains disciplined yet deeply human.

Individually, these tools are useful. Together, they form a living operating system—a way of leading that outlives any one person and centers students in every decision.

This book does more than describe the tools. It invites you into a process that is both structured and adaptive. You will see how blurred responsibilities can be clarified, how overwhelming data can be distilled into a few key indicators, how meetings can become culture-shaping rather than time-draining, and how priorities can be turned into action instead of good intentions. You will discover that clarity is kindness, that focus is liberating, and that discipline is what makes hope sustainable.

Most importantly, you will see how FASCO keeps students at the center. In an era when adults can easily become consumed by compliance or distracted by competing agendas, FASCO flips the script. Students are not the end users of the system—they are the reason the system exists. Every layer of the organization exists to support their growth, well-being, and future.

The pages ahead are both practical and profound. They will challenge you to think differently, to lead with greater discipline, and to create a system where alignment and coherence are the norm, not the exception. They will also equip you with ready-to-use structures and language that can transform how your team works together.

As you read, I encourage you not only to study the tools but to practice them. Use them with your leadership team. Bring them into your leadership meetings. Let them shape how you coach and how you decide. Most of all, let them remind you that leadership is not about doing more—it is about doing the right things with focus and clarity so that students can thrive.

The journey to becoming a Fully Aligned Student-Centered Organization is not easy. But it is possible. And it is worth it.

This book is your invitation. Lean in. Take the next step. And let FASCO reshape the way you lead.

Michael Duncan, EdD
Founder
NorthStarK12

PREFACE

As so many revolutionary ideas do, it all started with a crisis.

You may remember reading, or perhaps even writing, that districtwide email in the spring of 2020: School is cancelled for an extended spring break. Those days off quickly became a month. Then the world scrambled to figure out what virtual work and online school looked like. Mask mandates. Vaccine development. Social isolation. Confusion and misinformation. Even worries about students' nutritional needs kept you up at night.

It's lonely at the top.

This simple cliché, which I heard from educational administrators over and over during those years, has become the springboard for a revolutionary school leadership management system. And like many things in our time, it began as the world shut down, forcing us to rethink everything.

As co-founder and CEO of a company that supports the education industry by creating better learning environments, I had a front-row seat to the isolation and pressure school leaders experienced in those days of lockdown. The fear and unknown put superintendents in a position where what little support from peers and the community you may have enjoyed in "the good old days" disappeared. You were forced to make decisions that impacted hundreds, or even thousands, of students and employees. You couldn't talk to board members about certain things. You couldn't talk to staff about certain things. Some topics were so sensitive and confidential that you couldn't even go to friends and family for encouragement.

And no matter what choices you made, someone was going to be angry.

THE FASCO EVOLUTION

During this time, I had been fortunate enough to be plugged into a confidential peer network for organizations similar to mine. This was a place where I could talk to those who not only understood my struggles but also celebrated my wins. It soon became obvious that there was a huge need for a similar support system for school administrators, especially with the forced isolation during the no-contact days.

So I approached the same training organization that had set up my support network, and together we introduced small peer-support groups for school administrators. The Education Leaders' Organization (ELO) was born with the mission to improve education by improving the quality of leadership in our schools. Since that time, the ELO community has helped dozens of district and building administrators experience the growth that comes only when you find common ground with other leaders.

As those groups evolved, we started getting deeper into discussions about ways to run school districts better. How to drive meaningful progress. How to avoid burnout. How to build confidence. Members tapped into this group of other like-minded professionals who offered many proven solutions to common problems. But we found that some problems had yet to be solved.

One thread we uncovered was a stunning lack of standardized operational structure in most modern school systems. From role confusion between district and building leaders to overworked administrators managing both compliance and strategy, this gap in processes and configuration takes an enormous toll on student outcomes and staff retention.

Even without a worldwide health crisis, school leaders told us they scramble every day to coordinate tasks, respond to conflicts, and somehow keep an eye on big goals like student performance and teacher retention. They may be doing everything they can, but still don't feel like all the pieces are in sync as they should be. As a superintendent, assistant superintendent, principal, vice principal, or other school leader, they feel out of alignment. The different elements of their management systems just don't work together to produce a smooth ride. Sound familiar?

That's when we began exploring operating systems that had been working in other industries for decades. As the ELO board researched these profit-focused structures, it became apparent that the foundational principles that worked for mid-century thought leaders could be modified to align with the very specialized needs of education.

The Fully Aligned Student-Centered Organization, or FASCO, is a revolutionary new system that fuses proven management tools together to form a clear and streamlined process of operations in your schools. This is something you've never seen before: a group of six proven strategies that, when combined, create an approach to educational administration that fills in the gaps left by traditional organizational management systems. The FASCO model meets the unique challenges you face every day in a fresh way. It maximizes your efforts by focusing on leading-edge student-centered strategies that the old, familiar systems and methodologies tend to overlook.

Years of research and experience in operational management have produced hundreds of tools for administrators. Some proved to be fads, quickly catching fire and burning out. Others have demonstrated their usefulness, carving a space in the management world that is there to stay. The FASCO system is made up of those shining operational stars, tying them together to create a one-of-a-kind resource for educational administrators.

APPLE OR ANDROID?

Have you ever experienced the frustrating complication of a group text when even one person is using a different platform than everyone else? If some are using iPhones and some Androids, a photo might come through at a ridiculously reduced resolution, or a message may even disappear into the ether. When it comes to operating systems, it works best if everyone is on the same platform.

The same holds true for your school's or district's operating system. Whether you have a few hundred students or a quarter million, the more people who are using the same language to move closer to your goals, the better chance you have of getting there unscathed.

You probably entered education because you loved to teach or to coach students, but now your days are swallowed up by adults' demands. Teachers, staff, parents, and board members all present different challenges that can divert your focus. Financial worries and instructional crossroads might conspire to derail key goals. It's no wonder the average superintendent is on the job for a surprisingly short period of time before moving on. The sheer scope of administration can be overwhelming.

It doesn't have to be that way.

Now, you might say, "Oh, we have tried this gimmick and that gimmick. There is just no way to get an organization with this many moving parts to work in harmony."

Whether you realize it or not, your district is already using some sort of operating system. It's likely either a legacy method that was implemented years ago and left on autopilot or a strategy that you and your team have worked hard to build. But ask yourself this: Are all parts of your system working in harmony, or are they a bit piecemeal? Are they truly doing what you need them to do across your scope of responsibility? Are you feeling aligned in every area, from transportation and food service to test scores and community engagement? If your answer is not a resounding yes, you owe it to yourself to take a hard look at FASCO. It's more than just another acronym; it's a solution to burnout, mediocre student outcomes, and wasted time.

Take something as common as a hiring decision. You have a vacancy for an assistant principal at the top-rated high school in your district. Applicants include a pool of extremely qualified professionals. Does your operating system efficiently provide the information you need to make the wisest choice, or do you spend your evenings sifting through data to answer specific questions? Do you and your team know instinctively whether a candidate's philosophy or background is aligned with your district, because you have clear priorities and goals? Hiring at this level is not only a management decision, but it's also fraught with political implications. Can you, without a doubt, bring in this new leader knowing the students in your district will be best served by your choice? It's a tall order.

When you weave together the threads of the FASCO system, you will craft a strong and resilient structure at every level of your district. Eventually, this foundational work will change everything about how you do your job. From making hiring decisions easier to pivoting when—not if—an earth-shattering crisis occurs, paying special attention to these six administrative areas results in a smoother, more agile execution in every facet of your organization.

None of these tools are revolutionary on their own. You may have heard some of these terms or might already use something similar. But what makes a Fully Aligned Student-Centered Organization powerful is how these tools work together, creating a shared language and structure that aligns your entire school system. This combination builds responsiveness, innovation, and long-lasting success that extends beyond individual leaders.

If your current situation feels like the demands are never-ending and the stakes are too high, you're not alone. The job is big. The responsibility is real. And the path forward isn't always clear.

What if there were a way to find clarity, focus, and sustainability—not just for your district but for you?

This book is about finding that path.

When you become a Fully Aligned Student-Centered Organization, you create a legacy that will far outlast you. One that will serve students, staff, and the community you love for years to come. So let's get started.

HOW TO USE THIS BOOK

W. Edwards Deming, the father of the quality movement, said this: "Every system is perfectly designed to get the results it gets." Think about that for a moment. Positive results mean your system is right for your situation. Lukewarm, or even poor, results are directly tied to operating structures and procedures that are not aligned to your precise needs.

Are you getting the results you want?

If you've ever felt like your team is constantly reacting, stuck in endless meetings, or making decisions that feel disconnected from what's best for students, you're not alone. These aren't leadership flaws—they're system problems. And systems can be redesigned. That's where this book begins.

Becoming a Fully Aligned Student-Centered Organization is a two-part tool. It provides concrete solutions for school and district leaders who recognize that something about the way they've always done things isn't working; those who are ready to lead differently.

Part 1 is a story, not of perfection, but of transformation. It follows Dr. Alicia Ramirez, a fictional but highly relatable superintendent, as she navigates the overwhelming demands of her role. Her character is a composite of real school leaders who have realized that "the way things have always been done" no longer works. In the midst of utter despair, she finds an unlikely hero in the form of a FASCO coach and fellow superintendent whose own success persuades her to make a life-changing decision. You'll experience the emotional and operational challenges Alicia faces, and how her perspective begins to shift as she's introduced to the foundational tools of a Fully Aligned Student-Centered Organization. As her real-life counterparts did, she finds these tools aren't magic.

They're practical, proven, and intentionally simple. And as Alicia begins to use them one by one, her team starts to find focus, alignment, and relief. A true transformation.

We get a ringside seat as Alicia opens *Becoming a Fully Aligned Student-Centered Organization* and begins to deliver a proven structure and empowerment for her team, in addition to better outcomes for students. And spoiler alert: In the end, *Becoming a Fully Aligned Student-Centered Organization* ensures her mission is fully integrated into the daily lives of students, staff, and community members as she continues to move the district forward.

Part 2 is a hands-on tutorial to guide you in implementing FASCO in your own organization. It provides a deep dive into each of the six tools introduced in Alicia's journey. By following the FASCO model, you'll start with one tool. Practice it. Then add another. Over time, these six tools—**Accountability Circle**, **Vitals**, **Later List**, **Rocks**, **Vision**, and **Methods**—will become second nature, helping your school thrive now and for generations to come.

Each chapter in Part 2 is designed to help you implement one of the six tools with your team. You'll find clear explanations, implementation steps, sample agendas, coaching questions, and templates. Whether you're leading a district, a school, or a department, these tools are designed to meet you where you are and to grow with you as your organization becomes more aligned and student-centered over time.

This detailed, step-by-step instruction manual makes it possible to take things at your own pace. Executing the tools one at a time allows you to find a firm footing while enjoying the benefits of alignment almost immediately. This layered change management approach also provides opportunities for instruction and conversations with your core team to ensure efficient and clear-cut buy-in from stakeholders.

You don't need to read the entire book before taking action. Some leaders start with the story in Part 1 to build belief and understanding, then use Part 2 as a playbook. Others jump straight into a tool from Part 2 based on what they need most—whether it's clarity of roles, data that actually drives decisions, or a way to prioritize without becoming overwhelmed. There's no wrong entry point. What matters is that you begin building one step, one tool, one conversation at a time.

Leading schools is never easy, but with the right tools designed to be used together, it's possible to stay focused on your mission and build something that lasts. FASCO isn't just a new way to talk about school leadership; it's a new way to organize it. By using this framework, you'll shift from firefighting to focus, from compliance to clarity, and from leadership that depends on individual heroics to leadership that lasts. This book is your guide to that shift and a blueprint for building something better—something that works.

PART 1
A TALE
OF TWO
DISTRICTS

THE LEADERSHIP BOTTLENECK

1

Dr. Alicia Ramirez sits at her desk, staring at the glowing screen. Her office is dark except for the pale light of her monitor as the blinking cursor stares back from the district's strategic plan. Her desk is cluttered with paperwork, empty coffee cups, and sticky notes—reminders of promises she's made and deadlines she can't afford to miss.

Her phone buzzes softly. It's a message from her husband, Luis. *Are you coming home? The kids waited as long as they could.*

Alicia lets out a heavy sigh and types: *Soon.*

But she knows it isn't true. She isn't anywhere near finished and has long since stopped pretending she'll get ahead. The strategic plan is due in four days. Forty-three emails still need responses. And tomorrow morning, there's another meeting with her leadership team. How did it get like this?

Alicia glances at the glossy photo on her wall of the championship volleyball team she had coached in the years leading up to her big promotion. The girls' smiles tug at her heart as she tries to call up those important connections, those feelings of victory. Lately, she has been anything but victorious.

TWO WEEKS EARLIER,
EDUCATION LEADERSHIP CONFERENCE

Alicia shifts in her seat at the back of a crowded breakout session at the regional education leadership conference. She should be paying attention, but her mind is on her phone—email notifications and text messages piling up faster than she can process them.

At the end of the session, she heads for the coffee bar, already thinking about slipping out early. But as she waits in line, she hears a familiar voice.

"Alicia? I thought that was you!"

She turns and smiles. Marcus Boyd, superintendent of a neighboring district, stands behind her with a big grin.

"Marcus!" Alicia says, surprised. "It's been forever. How are things in Hillcrest?"

"Honestly?" Marcus chuckles. "Better than ever. We've discovered something that has been game-changing this year. I've actually got time to think strategically again."

Alicia raises an eyebrow. "Time to think strategically? What's your secret?"

"We made some major adjustments. Focused everything around just a few key priorities and simplified how we lead as a team. It's been a lifesaver. I feel, well, lighter."

"Lighter," Alicia repeats, a bit wistfully. "That sounds like magic. Almost unbelievable."

"It's not magic," he says, "but it feels like it sometimes. Believe it or not."

Before Alicia can press him for details, Marcus is whisked away by another superintendent. She watches him go, her curiosity lingering.

Lighter. She can't remember the last time she felt that way.

THE WEIGHT RETURNS

Back in her district, the idea of lightness feels like a distant dream. The moment Alicia steps into her office, the pressures close in around her.

The cabinet meeting is tense, filled with competing priorities. Staffing shortages at the high school. Budget cuts at the elementary level. An upcoming board presentation on declining enrollment. The leadership team looks to her for solutions, and once again, she finds herself saying, "I'll handle it."

The to-do list grows longer.

Just get through the week, she tells herself. But there's always another crisis waiting.

THAT EVENING AT HOME

It's after midnight by the time Alicia walks into the house. Luis is sitting in his favorite chair, reading a book. He glances up with tired eyes.

"You missed dinner again," he says quietly. "Olive made pancakes with chocolate chips just how you like them. Logan aced his spelling test." His comments are extended without judgment; simply an attempt to connect, to draw her in. But it only makes things worse.

Alicia drops her bag by the door and slumps onto the couch. "I'm sorry. It's just—everything. There's too much."

Luis nods slowly. "I know. But it's beginning to show. You've been exhausted for weeks. You're not sleeping. You barely eat. Even the kids are starting to worry." What he doesn't say sits like a boulder in the middle of the room between them: When was the last time she gave a second thought to her marriage?

Alicia presses her fingers to her temples. She feels the weight of it all pressing down—her career, her family, the thousands of students depending on her decisions. She's spent her entire career in education, pouring her heart into the work, but now she wonders if it's all slipping out of her grasp.

"I can't let the district down," she says, her voice barely above a whisper. "The staff, the students, the community, they're counting on me. If I fail, I'm failing all of them."

Luis takes her hand. "You're not failing anyone, Alicia. But you can't carry all of this on your own."

Alicia doesn't answer. She stares at the floor, her mind racing as tears pool in her eyes. She's given everything to this job—her time, her health, even parts of herself she barely recognizes anymore.

Is this just how the job is? she wonders. *An endless cycle of overwhelming responsibility and the struggle to survive?*

She's given everything to this job—

her time, her health, even parts of herself

she barely recognizes anymore.

THE BREAKING POINT

The next day, Alicia wakes with a pounding headache. Her body feels heavy, and even the thought of getting out of bed is paralyzing. She closes her eyes and considers calling in sick—a rare luxury she hasn't taken advantage of in years. But instead, she pulls herself up, gets ready, and heads to work.

At her desk, the blinking cursor on her laptop continues to mock her unfinished strategic plan. The emails keep coming. The phone won't stop ringing.

She stares at the screen, her mind blank. *I can't keep going like this.*

For the first time, she recognizes that something has to change, because if it doesn't, she won't be able to go on.

FRIDAY NIGHT, HIGH SCHOOL GYMNASIUM

The bleachers rumble as parents cheer, their voices blending into a loud hum that fills the gymnasium. It's the district basketball rivalry—Lincoln versus Hillcrest—and the crowd is electric.

Alicia leans against the wall at the edge of the court, her eyes scanning the game while keeping an eye on Olive and her friends at the snack bar. But her mind is elsewhere. She told herself she'd come to relax, to enjoy something outside of work for once. Maybe even to connect with her daughter. But the weight of her unfinished strategic plan and a dozen unresolved issues pulls her focus back to her mental to-do list. To make matters worse, the harsh fluorescent lights are threatening to trigger her headache once again.

"Dr. Ramirez!"

Alicia looks up to see Marcus Boyd weaving his way through

the crowd. He's wearing a Hillcrest sweatshirt and juggling a plate of nachos and a large soda.

"Dr. Boyd," she says, managing a smile. "We've got to stop meeting like this."

He chuckles. "Hey, I like a good basketball game. Plus, I can't pass up the nachos here."

Marcus stops beside her, scanning the court. "How's Lincoln holding up?"

"Oh, I'm not sure what the score is," Alicia stutters, embarrassed to be found daydreaming.

"That's not what I mean," Marcus says. "I'm wondering how your district is holding up. How you are holding up. I'm sorry we didn't get to finish our conversation the other day."

Alicia shrugs. "We're hanging in there. Same story as always—too much to do, not enough time to do it. You know how it is."

Marcus raises an eyebrow. "I used to."

Alicia tilts her head. "What's that supposed to mean?"

"I'm serious. Things are really different for us now. Better. I'm not saying it's perfect, but I've finally got my evenings back, and my team is stronger than ever."

Alicia blinks, caught off guard. "Evenings back? That sounds like a fantasy."

"It's not," Marcus says with a contented sigh. "We've made some big changes. I'll tell you what—let's grab coffee next week, and I'll fill you in. I think you'll find it interesting. Maybe Tuesday morning?"

Alicia hesitates, intrigued but unsure. How in the world could she shoehorn one more commitment into her schedule?

"Come on," Marcus presses. "It's worth an hour of your time. Coffee's on me."

"OK," she says finally. "I'll hold you to it."

TO GO OR NOT TO GO?

On Tuesday morning, Alicia stifles a groan as she wakes up exhausted. She had tossed and turned for most of the night, worrying about a conflict between two school board members. The thought of stumbling out of bed early for coffee with Marcus practically suffocates her. What was she thinking? She does not have time to implement some sort of newfangled system for the district. She considers texting Marcus that she can't make their meeting, but as she reaches for the phone, Luis stirs beside her.

"Don't cancel," he murmurs. "Something has got to change, and maybe this can be the first step." *He is right*, she thinks. *Something has got to change.*

Alicia gets dressed, grabs her briefcase, and stops in front of their family portrait on her way to the garage. "We'll figure this out," she whispers to the image of the happy faces hung on the wall. "I promise."

The coffee shop is warm and cozy, filled with the soft buzz of conversation and the scent of fresh pastries. Alicia arrives a few minutes early and finds Marcus already at a table, a notebook and coffee in front of him.

"Punctual as always," he says, standing to greet her.

"I try," Alicia replies, sitting down. After the waitress takes her order, she gets right down to business: "So, what's this secret you promised me?"

Marcus grins. "It's not a secret. It's more of a shift in how we operate—"

"Wait, let me guess," Alicia interrupts, looking away. "A twist on Marzano or PLCs? I think we've been there and done that. I doubt revamping a system is going to solve my problems."

Marcus raises his hand. "Hold on. This is not an attempt to polish rusty old tools. It's something completely different;

a consistent language and methods that work together to keep everyone, from teachers to my staff, focused on the same things. I know it sounds like hyperbole, but it's transformed how we run the district. We call it becoming a Fully Aligned Student-Centered Organization—FASCO for short."

"FASCO?" Alicia repeats, raising an eyebrow. "Hmm, another acronym to remember? Don't we already have enough of those in our profession?"

Marcus nods. "I promise this one is worth remembering. FASCO is a collection of tools—things like Accountability Circles, Vitals, Processes, Rocks—that help us concentrate our time on what really matters. More importantly, it has given my entire team a shared structure, so we're aligned. It's not all on me anymore. Now, it's not perfection, but overall, decisions are clearer, priorities are sharper, and the whole organization is pulling in the same direction."

"And this has actually made your job easier?"

"Absolutely," Marcus says. "Before FASCO, everything was bottlenecked with me. I was trying to manage every problem, every project, every initiative. But it wasn't sustainable. I was burned out. Honestly, I didn't know how much longer I could sustain the pressure. Sound familiar?"

Alicia chuckles, shaking her head. "Too familiar."

Marcus leans back in his chair. "Well, it didn't happen overnight, but once we started using these tools, the work got lighter. We focused on fewer priorities, aligned our processes, and empowered the entire team. For the first time in years, I feel like we're not just surviving—we're thriving."

Alicia sits quietly for a moment, processing his words. Finally, she takes a sip of coffee and pulls out her laptop, ready to take notes.

"OK," she says slowly. "I don't think I've ever seen you

so fired up about something, so I'll hear you out. I'm not convinced this will change anything for me, but to be honest, things can't get much worse."

MARCUS EXPLAINS THE CORE CONCEPTS

Over the next hour, Marcus lays out how his district became a Fully Aligned Student-Centered Organization.

"The first tool is called the **Accountability Circle**," he begins. "This is a unique org structure chart that places the student always at the center, as opposed to a traditional org chart with the leaders as the focus. All our decision-making radiates out from there. It helps us define clear roles and responsibilities, so everyone knows their part in supporting students."

Alicia holds up one hand. "Hold on. Am I hearing this right? You mean every decision is seen through the lens of how it might affect the student?"

Marcus nods. "Yes, and doesn't that seem like the way it should have been done all along? I wish I had found FASCO years ago."

"OK, that part sounds interesting. What's next?"

"The second tool is called **Vitals**. We stopped obsessing over a hundred different metrics and focused on the few that truly matter. If these predictive key indicators are healthy, the district is healthy," Marcus says. "This changes the focus from lagging measures to getting ahead of vitals that actually improve outcomes."

Alicia's brow furrows as she considers the possibilities. "I can imagine this process not only freeing up time but also creating more student success. I guess that goes back to the Accountability Circle, right?"

"Absolutely," Marcus says. "It's all tied together. That's the point."

He continued: "This next tool might be my favorite. So you know how sometimes important projects get lost in the shuffle of the urgent? This cool thing called the **Later List** helps manage priorities without letting things slip through the cracks. When we stopped trying to solve everything at once and created a system to manage tasks, it freed us up to concentrate on solving the urgent issues."

Alicia grins. "I can see why that's your favorite. It's so easy to just skate along when you reach a big goal. All that success can distract you from moving forward."

"Yes," Marcus says, "And the next tool ties into that. You may have heard of the term **Rocks** in relation to identifying an organization's top priorities. After hearing from the school board, we chose a few big district priorities each quarter, our Rocks, and built everything around those. No more shifting gears every month. Everyone knows what matters most." Marcus takes a sip of coffee while Alicia catches up on her note-taking.

"Wow," she says, much to her surprise feeling a little pressure lifting. "How much time we could save by pinning down top priorities and not rehashing that every month!" She looks at her watch and gasps. "Speaking of time, I have a meeting with one of my principals in half an hour. I hate to rush you, but what's left?"

Marcus grins. "No problem. We're almost done. The fifth tool is called **Vision**. We got crystal clear about what success looks like—not just for our students, but for the district as a whole. We made sure it wasn't just a document on a shelf, but something that guides our work every day.

"And last but not least, the sixth tool is **Methods**. We identified our core processes—the ones that matter most—and documented them. Now, we have consistency and shared expectations across the district."

Marcus finishes, taking a final sip of his coffee. "It's simple but powerful. And the best part? The whole thing is scalable and sustainable. The success of the district doesn't rely solely on me anymore."

Alicia leans back, watching notifications stacking up on her screen. Back to reality.

"This all sounds great," she says, closing her laptop. "But I just don't have the bandwidth to add anything else to my schedule right now. Maybe we could talk again over summer break."

"That totally makes sense," Marcus says, "and is exactly what I said when I heard about FASCO for the first time. But consider this: FASCO doesn't add more tasks or totally upend the district. It focuses on what matters and getting everyone on the same page. And once you embrace that mindset shift, everything changes. Do you really want to put that off until it's more convenient?"

"Everything changes? That's a big promise." Alicia stands, her mind racing. "But I do trust your opinion, and I've never known you to exaggerate. Maybe one more meeting?"

Marcus smiles. "I appreciate your trust. The real beauty of FASCO is the one step at a time approach. If you would allow me to explain the principles behind the Accountability Circle, I think you'll understand how even this one simple change can make a huge impact on your productivity. How about meeting at my office next Tuesday at this time? I'll bring the coffee."

Against her better judgment, Alicia pulls her phone from her purse and creates yet another calendar meeting. She shakes Marcus's hand and heads for the door, wondering if she has made a mistake. But as she steps out of the coffee shop, there's a flicker of something she hasn't felt in a long time—hope.

TAKING THE FIRST STEP

MARCUS'S OFFICE, HILLCREST SCHOOL DISTRICT

Alicia steps into Marcus's office, glancing around at the framed pictures of students, awards, and a large whiteboard filled with scribbled notes. Marcus waves her in, motioning toward the conference table where a binder and a few printed handouts await.

"Welcome to my war room," Marcus says with a grin. "Are you ready to learn?"

Alicia chuckles, settling into a chair as Marcus hands her the promised cup of hot coffee. "I guess as ready as ever. But I only have a couple hours before my next meeting. I hope that's enough time for you to convince me this is worth it."

He pauses, tapping a pen against the table. "I know your time is precious, Alicia. That's part of the reason it's so important to me to share this with you. I appreciate your trust."

She pulls out her laptop, trying to ignore the barrage of notifications while Marcus begins.

"First, I need to tell you I understand your skepticism. When my FASCO coach began explaining the concepts to me, I almost immediately shut down. I had heard some of these phrases and systems before and knew none of them were revolutionary, especially for education administration. But here's the catch: None of these tools are revolutionary *on their own*. You'll probably recognize parts of each one. Most districts, and even organizations outside education, already use similar processes. What we have here is a unique combination of new approaches and tried-and-true strategies. And the best part? What makes FASCO powerful isn't the tools themselves; it's how they all fit together, creating a shared language that aligns the entire organization."

Alicia nods. "Shared language. I like that. You wouldn't even believe how much time I spend trying to translate ideas across all the areas I'm responsible for."

Marcus chuckles. "Oh, I definitely believe it. But what if I could show you a path to give everyone—teachers, staff, even the school board—a common way to talk about what we do and how we grow? It starts with how we think about our roles in relation to students. We do this with one of the most foundational pieces: the **Accountability Circle**."

Marcus picks up a piece of paper and hands it to Alicia. It's a familiar sight—a traditional organizational chart, with the school board at the top, followed by the superintendent, then district leadership, site administrators, and finally, teachers at the bottom.

"This is how most districts think of their organization," Marcus says. "It's functional. Clear. But it also sends a not-so-subtle message about hierarchy and power."

Alicia studies the chart. "I've never thought of our structure that way. But now that you mention it, this chart looks, I don't know, rigid somehow. Like everything funnels down from the top."

"Exactly," Marcus says. "And while we all know we're here for students, they barely show up in this chart. Progressive districts may footnote them at the bottom, but that's about it. What if we flipped that idea and put the student at the center? In direct contrast to most organizational structures, the FASCO model centers everything on the student, not the administration."

He pulls out a second graphic—a circle with a student at the center. Surrounding the student are concentric rings.

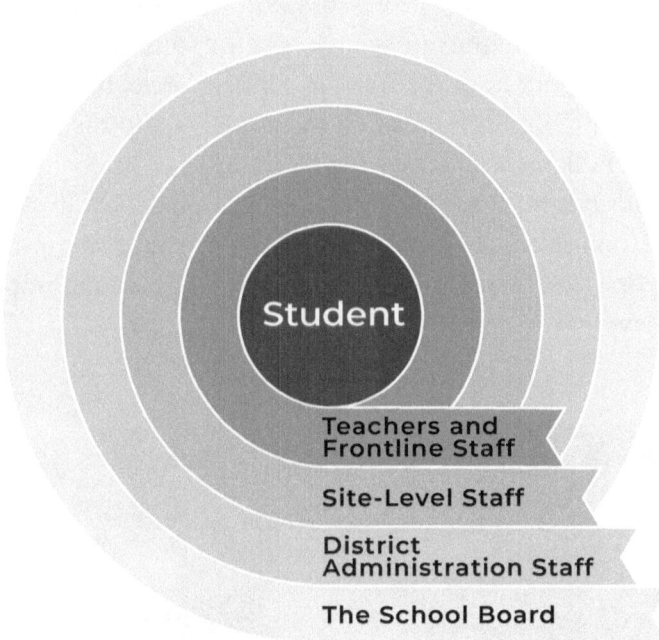

Student

Teachers and
Frontline Staff

Site-Level Staff

District
Administration Staff

The School Board

"This is the Accountability Circle," Marcus says. "The student is at the center, and every layer around them exists to support their growth. You can't argue with the fact that all your metrics improve if student instruction, health, security, and even inspiration are at their best. When students are happy, staff are happy. Community engagement goes up. Everyone wins when the students win. But here's the key: The student can't develop unless every layer of the circle is also growing and improving."

Alicia tilts her head, studying the image. "That's powerful. It feels more connected than the old chart. But it seems strange not to have teachers in the middle. I mean, there was nothing drilled into my head by my professors more than 'stay focused on your teachers and your district will be a success.'"

Marcus nods. "My professors said that, too. I'm not suggesting you start ignoring what's best for your teachers. But if you think about it, in the Accountability Circle, there is just a millimeter difference between the students and the teachers. Here at Hillcrest, when we began filtering decisions through the needs of students, it changed how we think about leadership and responsibility. Instead of seeing the district as a top-down structure, we started asking: "How do we grow and improve each layer of the circle so that students can thrive?"

> Instead of seeing the district as a top-down structure, we started asking: "How do we grow and improve each layer of the circle so that students can thrive?"

THE ROLE OF GROWTH IN EACH RING

Marcus points to the first ring surrounding the students. "Obviously, teachers are closest to the students. Their growth has the most immediate impact. It should absolutely be a top priority to make decisions that help support teachers. But as you know, there's a huge laundry list of possible ways to spend time and money where teachers are concerned. Would most of them be happy if you went to a four-day school week? Probably. But is that the best thing for student outcomes? That question needs to be answered before making any decision about teachers. Filtering every issue through a student-centered grid has made my life much less complicated."

Marcus pauses for a few seconds to allow Alicia to catch up on her note-taking before he begins tracing the next ring. "If you don't have any questions, let's move on. In order for teachers to grow, they need strong, supportive site staff—principals, counselors, and front-office teams who create the environment for great teaching and learning."

The new, energetic counselor at one of her middle schools jumps into Alicia's mind. This young lady has been on a mission to connect with students and makes it a priority to train other staff to do the same. Since the beginning of the year, student performance in that building has been going up, and discipline issues have been declining. Even the grumpy janitor has let up on his complaints. *Maybe Marcus is onto something here.*

Marcus is on a roll now, moving through each circle as his excitement builds: "For site staff to grow, they need clear guidance and strong systems from district staff. Things like curriculum support, professional development, and operational efficiency. And for the district to improve, the school board needs to be aligned and forward-thinking, ensuring that their decisions reflect the needs of every other layer."

Alicia nods slowly. "So, if any layer of the circle isn't growing, the student feels it."

"Exactly," Marcus says. "And along those same lines, if any layer of the circle is flourishing, so are the students. It's all connected. The power of the Accountability Circle is that it helps everyone see their role in student success, including their responsibility to grow so the students can, too."

CHANGING THE CONVERSATION

"We started using this visual in every conversation," Marcus continues. "It became a tool to reframe challenges. When a principal came to me frustrated about a new curriculum, we didn't just talk about implementation—we talked about what support the site needed from the district. When the school board pushed for higher test scores, we discussed how their decisions affected each ring of the circle and what resources were needed. And if someone wasn't flourishing in their role, we used a quick assessment called the ACE Test to make sure they were aligned, committed, and equipped for the seat they are in."

"The Accountability Circle gave us a common language," he adds. "And it shifted the focus from blame or top-down pressure to growth and support."

Alicia leans back in her chair, the idea sinking in. "I've never thought about it like that before. The traditional org chart never felt quite right, but I didn't know what to replace it with. This makes so much more sense."

"It does," Marcus says. "And once your team starts using it, it changes how they approach their work. Every decision, every initiative—everything starts with the question: How do we help each layer of the circle grow so students can thrive?"

A LITTLE HOMEWORK

Marcus hands her a printout of the Accountability Circle graphic.

"Take this back to your team—," he begins.

"Oh, hold on a minute," Alicia interrupts, dropping the paper like it's a hot potato. "Is this the point where I get homework? Don't let this info leave this room, but I don't even have my ninety-day plan ready for tomorrow's board meeting. I do not have time for one more thing." To drive her point home, she shuts her laptop and glances at her phone.

"I had the exact same reaction when I was in your place," Marcus says. "In fact, I had just found out my assistant super was moving across the state, and I was dealing with a board member's financial scandal and welcoming my third child into the world. It was not a good time for me either. Is it ever a good time?"

Marcus lets the question hang in the air as Alicia squirms. Her mind races as she mentally flips her calendar until finally realizing there is no break in sight. No stretch of time where she might take a leisurely look at her systems and processes. No time to reset anything. She thinks of the meme Luis texted when she decided to apply for the superintendent job: *If not now, when?*

"You're right," she sighs, picking up the paper once again. "What's my assignment, Coach?"

Marcus nods appreciatively. "You're gonna like this instruction: Start small. Use the Accountability Circle graphic in one conversation—maybe with your leadership team or a group of principals. Add it as a quick agenda item for a meeting you would be at anyway. Then ask your team what it would take to help each layer grow. You'll be surprised at the insights it brings out. And I guarantee, if you are feeling as stressed as you seem to be, those around you are feeling it as well. If they see you are looking for solutions, it will go a long way to energize them."

Alicia looks down, studying the graphic intently, hoping her stinging eyes won't betray her. "Ouch. I appreciate that brutal honesty and know it's true. I owe it to them to be a better leader."

"You already are," Marcus says. "Now, aren't you going to be late for your next meeting?"

WHAT MATTERS MOST 《 3

MARCUS'S OFFICE, THREE WEEKS LATER

Alicia settles into her chair, feeling a mix of relief and exhaustion. Across the table, Marcus leans in. "Tell me how it's going."

"Is it weird that I'm dreaming about FASCO?" she laughs. "Overall, it's been a whirlwind, but I think the Accountability Circle is starting to resonate with my team—at least most of them. Sheila, my veteran principal, who I rely on for a lot of wisdom, commented that focusing on kids has already made a difference in her school. They were considering making some big adjustments with scheduling, but after looking at how it would affect the youngest students, they opted not to implement the changes. It seems like centering on the students was something we always knew should happen, but we didn't quite know how to make the effort to change our thinking."

Marcus nods. "And has it been much of an effort?"

Alicia takes a beat. "You know, it hasn't been any sort of earth-shattering quick change. And I do have at least one person on my staff who isn't ever excited about change, so that has been a challenge. I think I caught him rolling his eyes at one point during our first Accountability Circle meeting."

"That's pretty typical of anything new in education, isn't it?" Marcus says. "But it sounds like you have the spark you need. It'll take time, but you've got that FASCO momentum going. It may even be embedded in your subconscious already since you're dreaming about it. So today, let's build on that forward motion with the next tool we call **Vitals**."

"Vitals?" Alicia raises an eyebrow. "Sounds serious."

Marcus chuckles. "It is. But it's also a lifesaver. Vitals are the few most important metrics that tell you if your district is healthy. Think of them like the key things a doctor checks—heart rate, blood pressure, oxygen levels. You don't need fifty data points to know if someone's healthy; you just need the right ones."

> You don't need fifty data points to know if someone's healthy; you just need the right ones.

THE PROBLEM WITH TOO MUCH DATA

Marcus grabs a marker and titles two lists on the whiteboard. One is labeled *Metrics We Track,* and the other *Metrics That Matter.*

"In most districts," Marcus explains as he scribbles, "we track everything—attendance rates, assessment data, discipline referrals, teacher evaluations, budget details, lunch participation, bus schedules, and the list goes on."

Alicia laughs. "You're not wrong. We have dashboards full of data, but half the time, it just feels like noise. Frankly, we all waste way too much time sifting through numbers. If you have a solution to that, I'm all ears."

"Well, Vitals has been a solid solution for us," Marcus says. "It's easy to get lost in all that data and miss what's really important. Vitals help you cut through the noise. It focuses your attention on the metrics that truly reflect the health of the district. If these are strong, you know you're in good shape. If they're weak, you know where to focus your energy."

DEFINING YOUR VITALS

Marcus circles the second list. "Now, let's think about metrics that really matter. Every district's Vitals are a little different, but they usually fall into a few key areas: academic achievement, student well-being, and operational health. Even though you have a thousand other things to track, these are the numbers you'd better never lose sight of."

He writes the following on the board: *1. Third-grade reading proficiency.* "At Hillcrest, our Vitals are simple. First, we concentrate on third-grade reading proficiency, because, as you know, that's a leading indicator for long-term success."

Alicia looks up from her notes. "Leading indicator? Can you refresh my memory of what that means in this context?"

"A leading indicator is a metric that tells us what is about to happen, versus a trailing indicator that documents what has already happened. For example, most school boards and administrators look at test scores at the end of the year. At that point, it's too late to respond if scores have declined, and they've wasted an entire year. So we keep close tabs on those reading assessment scores with weekly check-ins. If we notice a downward trend, we can intervene quickly. The idea is that if everyone has the most important leading indicators called out in front of them, we can actually manage and make adjustments if things start falling off track."

Alicia nods. "I suppose that also means you can celebrate and boost any upward trends as well."

"Exactly." Marcus continues to write on the board: *2. Student Attendance Rates.* "This is an obvious choice, because if kids aren't in school, they're not learning." He writes, *3. Teacher Retention*, and *4. Budget to Actual Alignment*, and then caps the marker and sets it down.

"That's it?" Alicia asks, surprised. "Just four metrics? How can that possibly be all you need to monitor?"

"That's it," Marcus confirms. "We have other data, of course, but these four tell us 90 percent of what we need to know. They're our primary focus and also an early warning system. If something's off, we dive deeper into the data to figure out why. But we don't waste time chasing a hundred different numbers."

Alicia's brow furrows. "And this is really working for you?"

"One hundred percent. I'm no longer staring at spreadsheets late into the evening or chasing down reports from my comptroller. Our board meetings are more focused and efficient, allowing members time to deal with those unexpected issues that always seem to surface. And the best part is that we are meeting and exceeding every educational goal," he says.

"Student-centered," Alicia says.

"Absolutely."

BRINGING VITALS TO LIFE

Alicia taps her pen against the table. "I like the simplicity of it. But how do you make sure these Vitals stay front and center?"

"We built them into everything," Marcus says. "Our leadership meetings start with a review of our Vitals. Every decision we make is filtered through them. And we share them openly with staff and the board, so everyone knows what we're focused on."

"Transparency," Alicia says thoughtfully.

"It is," Marcus agrees. "The best part is that it simplifies decision-making. Instead of getting pulled in a dozen directions, you have a clear way to prioritize. If a proposed initiative doesn't move the needle on our Vitals, we don't waste time on it."

"Once again, I feel like I'm about to get more homework," Alicia says, trying to ignore the threat of another headache. "Honestly, the thought of having to change gears right now is causing me a little anxiety. I can't imagine how to shift everything to a focus on just a few Vitals."

Marcus then opens his laptop and explains how the FASCO system provides an online tool called the Alignment Hub. This resource is designed specifically to support each of the FASCO tools, including (and not limited to) Vitals. It offers streamlined methods for identifying and tracking key metrics, including a rolling scorecard tailored for each organization's distinct needs.

"Start by identifying your own Vitals," Marcus says. "You probably have your eye on too many metrics right now—everyone does at first. Talk to your leadership team. Ask them: What are the key indicators that tell us if we're healthy as a district? If you can only track four or five things, what should they be?"

Alicia jots a note in her notebook. "Four or five. That'll be a challenge."

"It will," Marcus says with a smile. "Making that list will take a little more time and effort than implementing the Accountability Circle. And those Vitals are different for every district. But once you get them in the spotlight, it'll change everything. The clarity it brings is worth the work. At least it certainly has been for us."

Alicia nods, already thinking about her upcoming cabinet meeting. "This could really help us focus. I think most of my team will appreciate the simplicity—especially after the chaos we've been through lately."

"Even your eye-roller can't argue with a system that makes his job easier, right?"

Alicia chuckles. "That's a good point. And I have to admit I am still a little bit of an eye-roller myself at this point, but I appreciate your persistence with me."

"Patience is key," Marcus says. "Like any big change, this will take time to get buy-in from all your stakeholders. I'm still working on a few objections from my team. But overall, they can see how these adjustments are making steady improvements throughout the whole Hillcrest system."

THE POWER OF FOCUS

As she heads out for Logan's band concert, Alicia reflects on the conversation. For so long, her job has felt like a constant juggling act—balancing endless priorities and trying to make sense of overwhelming data. Cycling through spreadsheets and meetings like it's always Groundhog Day.

It's evident she needs something different in terms of metric measurements for herself, her team, and her students. That something might just be the focus that Vitals promises to provide. But as she pulls into the school parking lot, the skeptic in her keeps trying to surface. How can such a simple principle make such a big impact? Then she remembers the steady confidence she has observed in Marcus as their coaching sessions have progressed. His success is definitely an inspiration. She steps out of the car with a smile and a sense of purpose.

She can feel it—FASCO's Vitals is the next step toward real clarity. It's not about doing more; it's about doing what matters most.

NO MORE FIRE DRILLS

4

ALICIA'S OFFICE, MONDAY MORNING

Alicia sits at the head of the conference table, pen in hand. Although she encourages her team to put their devices away during their weekly meetings, Luis is out of town, and Olive is home sick today, so Alicia's phone peeks discreetly out from under her notebook. Across from her, her leadership team—principals, department heads, and senior staff—are flipping through notes, preparing for another packed week.

As usual, Alicia begins the meeting by asking each team member to share at least one win from the previous week. The curriculum director gives a glowing report of a conference she has attended featuring upcoming authors and publishers. The facilities director is encouraged, as he has unearthed a new paper supplier that would cut their costs substantially. Many other successes are celebrated as Alicia grows more and more nervous about the next agenda topic.

Finally, she takes a deep breath and looks around the room. "So," she says, leaning forward, "now that we've had a few days to sit with the idea of **Vitals**, what are your thoughts?" Their previous meeting resulted in a preliminary list of fifty top-priority metrics, so clearly they still have work to do. Alicia struggles to keep from looking directly at John, her eye-roller, who is uncharacteristically quiet this morning.

There's a pause before Sheila, the veteran principal, speaks first. "Honestly? I like it. The idea of narrowing our focus to a handful of key metrics makes sense. We've been drowning in data, and this forces us to zero in on what actually matters. I actually closed out a number of open tabs on my computer last night, and it felt great."

Nods around the table.

"I agree," adds Mark, the middle school principal. "But the challenge is picking the right ones. What if we leave something out that's important? Especially something that might get tagged as a requirement for our Title 1 funding."

"That's a fair point," Alicia says. "We're not looking to ignore everything else, but we need to recognize that we can't measure success by tracking fifty different things. If our Vitals are strong, our district is strong. If one starts slipping, we know exactly where to focus our attention."

More nods.

Then John, the high school vice principal, speaks up. Of course he does. "I don't understand how this will work. How can we resist the urge to keep adding to the list? We're all guilty of it—something comes up, and suddenly it's another 'top priority.' Eventually, it's just going to get cluttered up again."

The room falls silent as Alicia's team waits to see how she will handle John's pushback.

She breaks the tension with a smile. "John, thanks for your honesty. It really seems like we run from fire drill to fire drill sometimes, doesn't it? What if I told you that FASCO has a way to keep that from happening? As a matter of fact, it's our next tool—the **Later List**."

INTRODUCING THE LATER LIST

Alicia grabs a marker and moves to the whiteboard. She draws two columns:

Now | Later

"Here's the reality," she says. "There will always be more problems than we can solve at once. The Later List is how we manage what's important but not urgent—so we don't lose sight of it, but we don't let it distract us either. Let's look at some possible ways to prioritize a few things from the list of action items we brainstormed last time. And by the way, these are just working examples, so please don't get sidetracked by which topics I'm using."

She tries to avoid eye contact with John as she begins to create a list under *Now*:

- Teacher retention strategies
- Curriculum pacing adjustments
- Addressing chronic absenteeism

Then, under *Later*, she adds:

- New STEM program expansion
- Facility upgrades
- Adjusting high school start times

She turns back to the group. "Hopefully, you can see that the Later List isn't where ideas go to die. It's where they go to be **reviewed, prioritized, and acted on when the time is right**. Each week, we'll review this list in our Weekly Huddle. We'll rank items based on **importance and urgency**—some will move to *Now*, and others will stay put until we have the time, resources, or alignment to tackle them properly."

MANAGING THE WEEKLY HUDDLE

As if she can read Alicia's mind, Sheila steers the conversation away from potential complaints before things can be fully explained. "So, what exactly happens in this Weekly Huddle?"

Thank you, my friend, Alicia thought. "Great question," she says. "It's short and structured. We don't need another two-hour meeting. Every week, we do three things: First, we **review our Vitals**. Are we trending in the right direction? If not, what adjustments do we need to make?

"Second, we **check the Later List**. This is where we move any missed or off-track Vitals identified in our first step. Then we dive into what's happened over the past seven days: Has anything changed that makes one of these items a priority now? I think we can all remember how our focus made a seismic shift during the pandemic. This weekly check-in process keeps us poised to pivot more gracefully in times of crisis.

"And finally, we work through the Later List with an organized system of determining when it's time to **CLEAR** something from the list, moving it from the waiting room to the operating room, so to speak. At this phase, we're identifying what might be slowing us down and who needs additional support. And, before we begin, I want to emphasize that one important principle of this FASCO system as a whole is that it's never focused on blame, but on finding solutions as a team."

She gestures at the board. "So, we're no longer trying to solve everything at once. We're concentrating on what's most important while keeping an eye on what's coming next. This is how we become a high-functioning organization. Isn't that what we all want?"

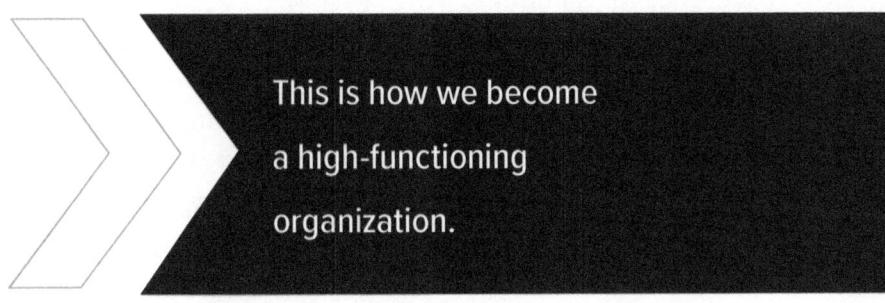

This is how we become a high-functioning organization.

PUSHBACK AND BUY-IN

John crosses his arms. "I like this in theory, but let's be honest—we all know how things go in education. A new crisis pops up every week. Even with the Later List, how do we keep from shifting priorities constantly?"

Alicia nods. "That's exactly why this system works. Right now, we react to everything. Through this FASCO tool, we can be more **proactive**. If something new comes up, instead of dropping everything, we put it on the Later List, **rank it**, and decide if it's urgent enough to move up to discuss and solve for now."

Mark leans forward. "So, it forces us to pause before we just say, 'Drop everything and deal with this.'"

"Exactly," Alicia says. "It keeps us from making emotional, reactive decisions that throw us off course. And I need to take this time to apologize to you all for how I have tended to manage from a reactive position. I have realized recently that jumping from crisis to crisis is no way to manage a school district, and that my policies in the past may have created more stress for you. I'm thankful the FASCO system crossed my path and hope it will reduce pressure and increase the potential for excellence for all of us."

The room falls silent as Alicia's team processes her heartfelt apology.

Finally, Sheila smiles. "You know, the Later List reminds me of how we teach kids to prioritize their work. We don't want them to panic and do everything at once. We tell them to focus on what's important now and plan for what's next."

"That's the idea," Alicia says. "It gives us a shared process for handling priorities—so we're not just reacting, we're leading. And I acknowledge it also gives us many opportunities for conflict. But if we can handle true conflict in a productive manner, this is when we will actually solve issues."

She pauses for that truth to sink in as heads begin to bob in agreement.

Alicia goes on to draw on the board a core principle of the Later List: *CLEAR.*

C   Identify the **C**ore issue

L   **L**isten to stakeholders

E   **E**xplore possible solutions

A   **A**gree on the best path

R   Determine who's **R**esponsible

"This stands for a process used to remove, or clear, any item from the Later List. Any item **CLEAR**ed will result in an action due within seven days," she explains.

John remains silent but picks up a pen and starts taking notes at this point. Alicia watches as each of her team members studies the CLEAR process, hoping they are picturing their own pet projects being prioritized in this logical manner.

THE NEXT STEPS

Alicia caps the marker and steps back to her seat. She glances down as her phone lights up with a message from Olive: *Feel better after my nap. Love u.* She grins at the uncharacteristically mushy message and tries to refocus on her team.

"Our time is about up for today, but I want each of you to bring your own Later List ideas to our next Weekly Huddle. Think about the challenges that have been lingering—the ones that aren't urgent but also aren't going away. We'll rank them together and start making this part of how we work."

The team nods, and Alicia can feel the shift in the room. There's still skepticism, but there's also a sense of relief.

Because for the first time in a long time, they have a way to manage what's coming without feeling overwhelmed by it.

A MOMENT TO PAUSE

5

Alicia sits on the living room floor, wrapping the last of the holiday gifts, while the sound of her kids laughing in the next room makes her smile. The scent of cinnamon and pine lingers in the air, and she glances out the window to see huge snowflakes falling from the dreary December sky. Before her stomach can clench for worry about whether or not she'll need to call a snow day, she remembers it's winter break. Taking a deep breath, Alicia realizes for the first time in a long time that she feels present. Not on constant alert, not moving from crisis to crisis, but simply there, enjoying the home she and Luis were building together. Enjoying her life.

As it should be.

It had been months since Alicia had been truly able to disconnect from work. Every break before this one had been filled with answering late-night emails, scrambling to finish reports, and popping antacids to cope with the worry of what awaited her when she returned. But this time was different.

Not perfect. But different.

As she leans back against the couch, she notices her laptop gathering dust on the side table right where it has been sitting, untouched, for days. Against her better judgment, she reaches for her phone. A single text from Marcus sits at the top of her notifications: *Enjoy the break. The work will still be there when you get back.*

She smirks, shaking her head. *He's right. It will still be there. But at least now, I have a way to manage it.* Then she tosses the phone aside and heads for the kitchen, calling, "Who wants to bake sugar cookies?"

SNOWMAN OR SANTA

Later that evening, Luis walks into the room with a steaming mug of tea in each hand and sits down beside Alicia, who's snuggled under a warm blanket.

"Snowman or Santa?" he says, offering her a choice of mug.

"Hmm. Since I still have sticky tape residue on my fingers, I think I'll go for Santa in his honor," she says. "Thank you."

The roaring fire Luis had built during the cookie-baking session is slowly burning down. The kids are in the other room enjoying their daily screen time, and things are uncharacteristically quiet.

After a few minutes, Luis tears his eyes away from the hypnotic orange embers and faces Alicia. "You seem different," he says gently.

Alicia exhales. "I feel different."

"Work finally slowing down?"

She laughs. "Not even close. But I think, well, I'm handling it better. I don't feel like I have to control everything anymore. I guess maybe I've realized that's a losing proposition."

Luis nods. "That's a big deal for you."

Alicia nudges him playfully. "I know." She pauses, staring at the Christmas lights flickering across the tree. "It's still a work in progress. The team is adjusting slowly, and I don't think John will ever buy into anything I propose, but I think most of them are convinced we're onto something. It seems counterintuitive, but this new FASCO system is even allowing me more time to concentrate on things outside of work. And to be honest, for a while last year I didn't know how much longer I could go on doing things the same way; how much longer any of us could."

Luis nods. "I believe it."

"I can't remember a time when I've been this refreshed. As a matter of fact, I think 'snowman or Santa' was the only decision I had to make all day."

"Ah, well, next time I'll choose for you, and you can relax even more." Luis sips his tea. "You know, the kids noticed you were home more this week."

Alicia looks up. "Really?"

"Yeah. Logan said you actually sat and watched a whole movie with them without looking at your email. I think he was in shock."

Alicia chuckles but feels a lump in her throat. Had she really been checked out for that long?

Luis reaches for her hand. "I don't need you to change the world, Alicia. I just need you to remember that you're allowed to breathe."

Maybe for the first time in her career, she actually believes it.

She squeezes his hand, taking in the moment as Olive and Logan burst into the room. "We want to go sledding," Olive declares. "Who's in?"

Luis looks at Alicia, eyebrows raised. "You coming?"

"You guys go ahead. I'm way too comfortable here in front of this warm fire."

LOOKING BACK

"Don't stay out too long!" she calls as the door slams. In the stillness, her mind drifts back over the past few months. Has FASCO really made a permanent shift in her work habits and given her a second wind for her career? Or is it too good to be true?

As the doubts assail her and threaten to ruin the peaceful moment, Alicia begins to consider everything from a purely empirical perspective.

The Accountability Circle absolutely reframed how her team thought about their roles. Instead of a top-down org chart, they started seeing themselves as part of a structure designed to grow together, with students at the center. Morale was up, complaints were down, and there was a clear uphill trend with testing scores. Yes, it was clearly making a difference.

Vitals had helped them focus on what truly matters. They weren't getting lost in a sea of data anymore. They had clear indicators to measure the district's health. She still had some doubts about leaving out an important bunch of numbers, but Marcus had assured her that any of those discrepancies would quickly become evident.

The Later List gave them a way to manage what was important but not urgent. It had already saved them from chasing a dozen distractions. True, it created some discord about how to CLEAR their list, but that was to be expected. The difference of opinions will always be there.

Not everything had gone smoothly. There was still skepticism, and honestly, she wondered if the next few FASCO principles would continue to make a difference. Some staff members were waiting for this to fade like every other initiative.

But Alicia could feel the shift. Her leadership team was actually learning to think differently.

She had been learning, too.

She wasn't taking every problem on her shoulders, but rather giving her team space to lead. And for the first time in years, she had allowed herself to step away—even if only for a few days.

A NEW YEAR, A NEW CHAPTER

The Christmas tree was at the recycling center, decorations put away, thank-you notes written, and a mishmash of leftover cookies and candy littered the kitchen counter. One more day of peace and quiet before the district offices reopen. Alicia wraps one hand around the mug of hot chocolate—snowman this time—and opens her notebook with the other.

Alicia knows there's still a long road ahead. There will be challenges, pushback, and moments of frustration. But for the first time in a long time, she's stepping into the second half of the school year with clarity.

She flips to her notes from her last meeting with Marcus.

Next up: **Rocks**. Focused and measurable. The kind of thing she can really get behind. She just hopes her team feels the same way.

She takes a deep breath. "One step at a time."

A NEW CHALLENGE

6

Alicia steps into her office, the quiet of winter break already a distant memory. The inbox she had carefully ignored over the holidays is now overflowing, and the day's calendar is stacked with back-to-back meetings.

She takes a deep breath and reminds herself: one step at a time.

Just as she sits down to check emails, Pam, her director of curriculum, appears in the doorway, dark rings under her eyes and her normally perfect blond curls in disarray. "Back to reality," Pam quips, but the tension in her voice is unmistakable.

Alicia smiles, thankful she had time to stop for coffee on the way in. "We sure are. How was your break?"

"Oh, it was fine," Pam says. "We all have sugar hangovers, and I spent my last free day returning gifts, but it was good. But, Dr. Ramirez, we have a problem."

Alicia takes a sip and sets her coffee aside, meeting Pam's eyes as she leans across her desk in solidarity. "Of course we do. What is it?"

Pam hands over a report. "I just got attendance numbers from the last week before break, and things are still dropping. Overall, we're down six percent from last year at this point. I think this is moving beyond what we can handle in the Weekly Huddle. It might be time to transfer the problem of falling attendance from the Later List and take action before things get any worse."

Alicia scans the numbers, her stomach tightening. Chronic absenteeism had been an issue before, but this was a sharp decline. Thank goodness their Vitals caught the problem in its early stages when something could be done to reverse its course.

"Any idea what's causing the issue?" Alicia asks.

"We're still digging into things," Pam says. "But from what I'm hearing, there are multiple factors—illness, disengagement, transportation issues. And some of our families are still struggling from the economic ripple effects of last year."

Alicia rubs her temples. "So, not a simple fix."

Pam shakes her head. "Definitely not."

Alicia exhales slowly. This is exactly the kind of problem that derails districts. It's important. It's urgent. But it's also complex.

A few months ago, she would have called an emergency meeting, dropped everything, and started tackling the problem herself. She would have missed Olive's winter recital and stuck Luis with all the parenting duties once again. But she knew better now. This is just the kind of multifaceted situation FASCO was designed for.

"We'll bring this into our quarterly planning meeting," Alicia says. "Let's not jump to solutions yet—let's put everything on the table and decide how to approach it strategically."

Pam looks relieved, catching a glimpse of herself in the mirror and tucking a stray curl behind her ear. "That makes sense. We can't fix it overnight, but we need to get ahead of it before it gets worse."

Alicia nods. "Exactly. Let's get this on the agenda for the leadership team meeting, and we can start working on a plan together."

LET'S BE HONEST

Two days later, the leadership team gathers around the conference table. John stirs a steaming cup of hot chocolate with a stale candy cane. Everyone has been briefed on the attendance slump. There's an energy in the room that was not there the last time they met—not quite panic, but a shared understanding that something needs to shift.

"Before we dive into absenteeism," Alicia begins, "let's take a step back and assess where we are. It's been ninety days since we started using the Accountability Circle, Vitals, and the Later List. Let's be honest. What about FASCO is working so far, and what's still a struggle?"

There's a brief silence as Alicia makes eye contact with Sheila, willing her to set a positive tone. Some of the few messages Alicia replied to over the break were from her stalwart teammate, thanking her for having the courage to initiate such sweeping changes. For the first time in years, Sheila was also able to enjoy her family over the holidays.

Sheila raises her hand and, with a nod from Alicia, begins the discussion. "Vitals have been a game changer. Having a few key metrics has made it so much easier to focus our discussions at the school level. My teachers and staff are becoming big FASCO fans."

Dan, the high school principal, nods. "Same here. I used to feel like we were drowning in data. Now, we're actually using it instead of just reporting it. That online dashboard has also saved us a ton of time. What's it called again?"

"The Alignment Hub," Pam says, jumping into the discussion. "It is a super useful tool. I think someone on my team uses it nearly every day."

A murmur of agreement ripples around the table.

Pam adds, "The Later List has been helpful, too. It's stopped us from trying to tackle everything at once. But I'll admit, it's hard to leave things on the list and not feel like we're ignoring them."

Alicia smiles. "That's exactly why we're here today. The Later List isn't there so that we can ignore things. It's a tool that will help us determine when the time is right to address things. And today, we're going to decide what moves from **Later** to **Now**."

She gestures to the board, where two columns are already filled in.

Now | Later

Under **Later,** absenteeism tops the list. Other items include:

- Expanding mental health support
- Revisiting school start times
- Updating teacher professional development structures
- STEM program expansion

Alicia picks up a marker. "The next step is to move some of these into our quarterly priorities—our **Rocks**."

TURNING PRIORITIES INTO ROCKS

Marcus's words echo in her mind: "If everything is important, nothing is."

Alicia turns to the team. "Here's how we're going to do this. We can't fix everything in one quarter, but we can focus. We'll pick three to five priorities—the big Rocks we commit to solving over the next ninety days. But first, let's have a little show and tell."

She reaches down under the table and pulls out a box, placing it in front of her. From the box, she pulls a large jar, a bag of sand and one of pebbles, three larger stones, and a pitcher of water. "Let's say this jar is our school year, the whole nine months represented by this beautifully empty space. These rocks are, obviously, the most important goals for the year. The things that should be determining where everything else fits. But what if we get excited about the pretty pebbles and put them in first?" Alicia dumps the pebbles in the jar. "Then the sand seems like something easy to work in, so let's do that next." She dumps the bag of sand in the jar, filling it past the halfway point.

"I see where you're going with this," says Sheila. "Now that the small things are in the jar, the rocks won't all fit."

"Exactly." Alicia beams. "Gold star for Sheila. If we don't give big goals our primary focus, all the little details and crises of the year will crowd them out." She turns the jar over, dumping the sand and pebbles back in the box and replacing them with the large rocks. Next, she picks the pebbles back out of the box and drops them in the jar. Then, the sand. Her team is quiet as she reaches for the pitcher of water, dumping it over the contents of the jar and filling each space perfectly. "If we start with our major issues, everything else will fill in around them."

A smattering of applause ripples around the room as Alicia turns to draw another heading on the board: **Quarterly Rocks**. The conversation begins.

Pam pushes for absenteeism to be a priority. "If we don't address this, everything else suffers."

Dan argues for mental health support, saying teachers are noticing increased anxiety and disengagement among students, which also plays into absenteeism.

Sheila advocates for professional development, pointing out that teachers need time to reflect, collaborate, and adapt. *Sheila can always be counted on to think of other people. That's what makes her such an excellent leader,* Alicia muses.

John, surprisingly, is silent. But his hot chocolate has made a complete mess of the table.

The exchange is productive, Alicia communicating clear expectations of starting points and goals for each issue in order to keep the focus on progress. She deftly counters any attempts to place blame, highlighting instead any positive steps that can be taken to solve issues. By the end of the meeting, they land on four Rocks:

1. **Reduce chronic absenteeism from 6 to 3 percent**—Focus on data analysis, outreach, and school-level interventions.
2. **Implement district-wide mental health support plan**—Define and roll out a structured wellness initiative across all schools, integrating mental health resources and tracking impact on student attendance and engagement.
3. **Design and launch a professional development pilot at elementary schools**—Shifting to job-embedded, collaborative learning aligned with teacher-identified needs.
4. **Investigate secondary school start time adjustments**—Complete research, stakeholder engagement, and scenario modeling to determine viability of adjusting start times for improved student outcomes.

Alicia circles the list. "These are the priorities we're committing to for the next ninety days. Everything else stays on the Later List until the next quarter."

ASSIGNING ACCOUNTABILITY

She looks around the table. "One more thing—each Rock needs a single point person. This doesn't mean you do all the work, but it does mean you own the Rock and give a weekly update on whether it's on track or off track."

Pam raises her hand. "I'll take absenteeism. It ties directly into curriculum and engagement, and I'm already working with data teams."

Dan speaks up next. "I can lead the mental health initiative. Our counselors have been pushing for more structure, and I can pull them in."

Sheila nods. "I'll own teacher PD. If we don't get this right, nothing else will stick."

Alicia jots down their names next to each Rock, then turns to Mark, the middle school principal. "Mark, would you take school start times?"

He hesitates. "I can, but why me?"

"Because middle school families will be impacted the most," Alicia says. "You're in the best position to lead the conversation with stakeholders."

Mark nods slowly. "Fair point. I'm in."

Alicia smiles. "Great. Each of you will check in on your Rock during our Weekly Huddle. If it's on track, say so. If it's off track, let's talk about why and how we fix it. No surprises."

As the meeting wraps up, Alicia turns to the group. "We'll meet again in three months for another quarterly planning session—"

"And it'll be spring break time, baby," John interrupts, sloshing hot chocolate on the table.

Sheila ignores him and nods to Alicia. "Ninety days is the right spacing. It will keep us focused but also give us time to make progress. I think if we go too long without checking in, things will start to drift."

Pam smirks. "You mean we go back to running around putting out fires?"

"Exactly," Alicia says. "But not anymore. This keeps us aligned, no matter what comes our way."

She looks around the table. "Does everyone feel clear on what we're tackling?"

Heads nod. There's still a lot to do, but the chaos feels contained. They have a strategy and the talented people to make things happen.

As the team heads out, Alicia lingers for a moment, cleaning up the sticky mess John left behind on the conference table. Ninety days. One step at a time. She picks up her phone and texts Marcus: *Quarterly planning done. Rocks set. Feeling focused.* A few minutes later, his response pops up: *Good. Now stick to it.*

She smiles.

That's the plan.

THE UPS AND DOWNS OF PROGRESS

7

Alicia looks up from pouring her coffee as John saunters into the break room with a bag of microwave popcorn. "Hey, boss," he says and nods.

"Hi John," she replies. The microwave begins humming as she considers whether or not she has the energy to engage with him today. Finally, she dives in. "Hey, I have a question for you if you have a minute."

"I have time if you do, I guess," he says with a shrug.

"You were pretty quiet at that planning meeting the other day. I'm wondering if I can take that as at least a little buy-in on the FASCO system?"

"You can take it however you'd like," John says, not meeting her eyes. "I still think the whole thing will burn itself out eventually, just like every other management initiative we've tried. Frankly, it annoys me that we waste so much time and energy—and dollars—on the next magic cure for the district's problems."

Alicia sips her coffee and waits for him to finish. He always has more to say.

"And I'll tell you why I didn't speak up at the meeting," he says as the microwave dings. "Everyone who expressed excitement about something got more work to do. Simple. He who speaks up gets assignments. I'm busy enough."

At least he's honest, Alicia thinks as she tries to come up with a response that won't make things worse. "I do hear your concerns, John. I've had the same hesitations, and some days still doubt that this will make a difference in the long run. But as my FASCO coach says, we have to trust the process. I ask that you hold your final judgment for a bit longer."

"I guess I don't really have a choice, do I?" John says.

"You always have a choice, John," she replies, struggling to keep her temper in check. "And I would hope you choose to be a team player and remember the focus of the Accountability Circle. Does your skepticism serve the students or get in the way of their success?"

Without answering, John glances at the clock and gives Alicia a mock salute as he heads for the door. "About time for our next meeting, boss."

EXCAVATING MORE LAYERS

Alicia walks into the conference room for the weekly leadership huddle, glancing at the board where their quarterly Rocks are listed with a "please do not erase" note for the custodian. It's been about six weeks since they set their priorities. Enough time to know whether progress is happening or not. She's eager—and a little nervous—to hear how things are going.

She kicks off the meeting right on time, knowing that if they don't stick with the agenda, she will be late picking Olive up for her dentist appointment. "All right, let's check in. We'll go around the table, and I'll ask you to tell us if your Rock is on track or not. If it's off track, what's the challenge? So we'll start at the top: Rock number one is 'reduce chronic absenteeism from 6 to 3 percent.'"

Pam clears her throat. "We're making some progress. But not enough."

Alicia picks up a pen. "What's holding us back?"

"We've identified our most at-risk students, and the outreach efforts are helping. But the transportation issue is a bigger deal than we thought. A good portion of our absences is tied to students not having a reliable way to get to school."

Dan nods. "Same story on my end. We've had kids missing first period regularly because their parents work early shifts, and buses are full. If we don't fix the transportation gap, I don't know how much more we can move the numbers."

Alicia exhales. *Not a failure—just a new layer of the problem.*

"OK," she says. "Thank you both for your diligence here. Let's flag transportation as a separate issue. Pam, you're still accountable for absenteeism, but we might need to move that part of the challenge onto the Later List for next quarter."

Pam nods, relieved. "That makes sense."

"Let's move on to Rock number two: Launch a mental health support plan," Alicia prompts.

Dan leans forward. "Good news on this one. We've developed a structure and piloted it at two schools already. Counselors are leading small-group check-ins with students, and feedback has been great. Teachers are reporting fewer behavior disruptions in the classes where students are participating."

Alicia smiles. "That's fantastic. Are we ready to expand it?"

"Almost," Dan says. "We need more staff training, but we should be able to scale district-wide next quarter."

"Thank you, Dan. I look forward to hearing your next update. Now, let's move on to Rock number three: Pilot a revamped teacher PD model. Based on the focus of the Accountability Circle, I have to say I am happy to see this made it to the Rocks list."

Sheila sighs. "Yes, I've been very excited to work on this. But I'll be honest—we are off track here."

"What's the holdup?" Alicia asks, not unkindly.

"We had the plan in place, but implementation has been rocky. Teachers are struggling with time constraints, and principals are balancing too many priorities. Even though they are really craving meaningful professional development, most are too overcommitted and exhausted to take advantage of it."

"I get it," Alicia says. "Does this model need to be reworked or just given more time?"

Sheila thinks for a moment. "More time. If we keep refining things, it'll work, but not overnight."

"Got it," Alicia says. "I'm sure Sheila would love input from more of our team if anyone here has time to meet with her." She tries not to look directly at John. "We'll roll this one into the next quarter with some adjustments."

Finally, the team focuses on Rock number four: Explore school start time adjustments.

Mark leans back in his chair. "Believe it or not, this is actually done."

Alicia's eyes widen as a smattering of applause echoes around the table. "Seriously? That's fantastic!"

"Yeah. After gathering stakeholder input and digging into the data, we decided not to change start times—at least not yet. The research showed mixed benefits, and the transportation impact would have been a nightmare. So, for now, we're pausing it."

Alicia nods, impressed. "That's progress. Deciding not to do something is just as important as deciding to move forward. Great work."

"Guess I should have raised my hand for that one," John mutters. Alicia ignores him.

BIG CHANGES ON THE HORIZON

As the quarter progresses, the team navigates the usual ups and downs—unexpected challenges, late-night board meetings, and budget revisions. But one major development shakes things up in a way Alicia didn't see coming.

One afternoon, Sheila walks into Alicia's office and closes the door behind her.

"I need to talk to you," she says, her tone unusually serious.

Alicia gestures to the chair across from her desk. "What's going on?"

Sheila sighs, tears gathering in the corners of her eyes. "I've made a decision. I'm retiring at the end of the school year."

Alicia feels her stomach drop as she inhales sharply. "Wow. I didn't see that coming."

"I know," Sheila says. "I wasn't planning on it this soon. But after thirty years in education, it feels like the right time. The grandkids are getting more and more active, and you know I've always wanted to travel. I want to make the move while I still have energy to enjoy retirement."

Alicia nods, collecting her thoughts as Sheila reaches for a tissue. Losing Sheila—one of her strongest leaders and best friends—is a big deal. Who else can she turn to who will understand the undercurrents of the leadership team and always offer her honest support? Sheila even gets all her jokes. She seems irreplaceable.

But instead of panicking, Alicia reminds herself that this is precisely why FASCO works. The district isn't dependent on any one person. *But am I?* She forces a smile. "I'll be honest, I don't want to lose you. But I respect your decision. We'll make sure the transition is smooth."

Sheila smiles. "I know you will. You've built something sustainable here, Alicia. That's part of why I feel comfortable stepping away. And I promise to send you a postcard from Cabo."

Alicia exhales. Maybe Sheila's retirement is the biggest sign of progress yet.

MARK YOUR CALENDAR

By the time they reach the last week of the quarter, Alicia knows what's next.

They'll celebrate the wins. They'll adjust to the challenges. And they'll set new Rocks for the next quarter.

But this time, they'll also be planning for something bigger.

At the final leadership meeting of the quarter, Alicia stands at the front of the room, clicking to a colorful *Congratulations, Sheila* slide. "You have probably all heard by now that Sheila will be leaving us at the end of the year. I would just like to take a moment to thank her publicly for her years of service and her countless contributions to the district and community. Personally, it's hard for me to say goodbye, but I'm so happy for the fun she'll have as an old, retired lady."

Everyone chuckles as they take Alicia's lead in applauding their colleague.

"All right, team. We've learned a lot over the last ninety days. We've had successes, we've had setbacks, and we've adapted along the way. But now, it's time to think bigger."

She clicks to the next slide: *Annual Planning: Two-Day Retreat, June 15–16.*

"Sheila, as your last leadership retreat, we hope to soak up all your opinions and wisdom before you take off into your future. We've blocked off two full days this summer to step back, reflect on the past year, and set a clear vision for the next. This is where we decide the big picture priorities for the next school year—not just for the leadership team, but for the entire district."

Sheila smiles. "This will be so much fun, and I promise not to check out yet. Ninety days is the right amount of time to make progress, but a full year? That's where we really move the needle."

Dan nods. "Where's this happening?"

"Offsite," Alicia says. "I want us out of the office, away from distractions. I'll send details soon, but for now, block your calendars. No excuses."

A palpable energy buzzes throughout the room as the team reaches for their calendars, smiles and nods all around. A sense of purpose seems to be powering their actions. Even John is unable to resist the urge to engage.

Alicia feels it, too.

For the first time, they aren't just managing a district. They're building something that will last.

A CLEAR VISION

8

The warm summer air drifts through the open windows of the conference room, a stark contrast to the usual fluorescent lighting and rigid schedule of district meetings. Today, there are no student emergencies, no last-minute fires to put out, no personal errands to run. Just Alicia and her leadership team, gathered for two uninterrupted days of reflection, planning, and forward-thinking.

She stands at the front of the room, a whiteboard behind her, as her team settles in. The table is stacked with old reports, past initiatives, and a binder labeled "Portrait of a Graduate—2018." Next to it is another document: "Master Plan Report—2020." *What a year that was.*

Alicia clears her throat. "Before we look forward, let's look back."

She gestures to the materials. "We've done great work in the past—crafted a Portrait of a Graduate, mapped out a long-term master plan in the midst of a worldwide crisis. But how much of that is actually guiding us now?"

The room is silent. The answer is obvious: not much.

RENEWED SENSE OF DIRECTION

"That's what today is about," Alicia continues. "We're not starting over. We're reconnecting to the big picture and setting annual priorities that will drive everything we do next year. We are building our Vision."

She clicks to her first slide: *Create the highest, grandest vision possible for your life, because you become what you believe. —Oprah Winfrey.*

Then, without comment, she moves on to the next slide: *The only thing worse than being blind is having sight but no vision. —Helen Keller.*

And the next: *Where there is no vision, the people perish… —King Solomon.*

As her team digests her inspiration message, Alicia moves to the board and writes three questions:

1. Where have we been, and where are we going?
2. What must be true for us to get there?
3. What will we commit to over the next year?

She turns back to the group. "I think normally we tend to jump to question three when planning Vision. But the first two questions are equally important. If we can answer all of these with some sort of cohesiveness as a group, we are well on the way to crafting a smart Vision. And, before we begin, please keep the Accountability Circle front and center. Every part of our Vision must be anchored to student success. Let's start with question one."

Pam flips through the Portrait of a Graduate document. "I'm really glad you brought these in so we can first see where we've been. When we created this years ago, it was supposed to be our North Star, documenting trailing indicators of student success. What factors must be in place to graduate a student who will become a successful, contributing member of their community? It was fun to compile these stories, and I love looking back at some of my favorite moments. But I don't think we've used it as much as we should."

Mark nods, flipping through the Master Plan. "Same with this booklet. We did all the hard work to design what our schools should look like over the next decade. But outside of a few facilities projects, it's kind of, well, honestly, it's just stalled."

Sheila, keeping her promise to share her wisdom, chimes in. "That's the challenge of school leadership—we do big, meaningful work, but we don't always build the systems to keep it alive."

Alicia picks up a marker before John can derail the conversation with his "I told you so" negativity. "So, team, let's change that. What parts of these documents are still relevant? What do we need to refine?"

Over the next hour, the group revisits their history, pulling the strongest pieces from past work and identifying gaps. Each leader has a chance to share their specific wins and challenges, and the group finds an unexpected sense of camaraderie as they connect with each other's struggles. Alicia's team emerges with a renewed sense of direction and a Vision of a future-ready district that is intentionally student-centered. Fully aligned.

"Great," Alicia says, smiling. "Let's take a quick break before moving on to question two."

SETTING ANNUAL GOALS

After a refreshing coffee break on the sun-soaked patio, the team heads back indoors.

They split into small groups, each tackling a different aspect of what must be true for them to succeed over the coming year. When they reconvene, Alicia writes their top themes on the board:

1. We need a shared system that keeps us aligned.
2. We need to actively involve all our staff in this work—not just leadership.
3. We need clear, measurable progress indicators.

She steps back. "So, this is where we want to be. Sound familiar?"

Pam grins. "This is exactly what we've been working toward with our Fully Aligned Student-Centered Organization."

"Exactly," Alicia says. "So, here's the real question: How do we embed FASCO across the district—not just at the leadership level, but everywhere? What must happen for our Vision to spread?"

The room falls silent as the weight of the question sinks in.

Then Dan speaks up. "We need a way to teach this to our entire district."

Sheila nods. "We've created tools, language, and systems that are working for us. But for this to last beyond leadership changes, beyond initiatives, we need to document it in a way that's accessible to everyone."

Alicia's eyes widen as the idea clicks. "What if we create a book?"

The group looks at her, intrigued. John avoids eye contact.

He's afraid that if he shows interest, I'll assign the book project to him.

"A short book," she continues. "A guide to becoming a Fully Aligned Student-Centered Organization. Something that explains the tools, the language, and how we use them as a district. It wouldn't just be for new hires; it would be for everyone. A common reference point, something that lives beyond meetings and presentations."

Pam leans forward. "I love it. It's not just another professional development session that people forget—it's a real, tangible resource."

Mark adds, "It could also help us train new leaders so we don't lose progress when someone retires or moves on."

Sheila raises a hand, "Guilty."Alicia smiles. "Exactly. Sheila, thank you for providing a great illustration of the point. If we want this work to outlast us, we need to make it tangible."

She grabs a marker and writes on the board:

Create and launch
Becoming a Fully Aligned
Student-Centered Organization
as a tool for all staff.

Heads nod. Even John seems to be on board.

After more discussion, they land on three goals that will drive their work for the coming year:

1. Document and share the FASCO model across the district.
2. Strengthen staff involvement in decision-making using FASCO tools.
3. Refine and integrate Vitals, Later List, and Rocks into school-level planning.

Alicia circles the goals. "These are what we will commit to for the coming year. They will guide our Rocks each quarter. Every major initiative should align with one of these."

She looks around the room, taking in the mix of excitement and determination.

"This is it," she says with a deep sense of clarity. "We're doing more than leading a school district. We're building a system that will shape how we work for years to come."

Sheila leans back in her chair. "That's how you know you're doing something meaningful. I'm so excited I just may put off my retirement."

Alicia chuckles, "Don't tease me like that."

Before they wrap up, Alicia turns to the group. "We've done the big-picture thinking. Now we need to stay on track."

She clicks to the final slide: *Next Annual Planning Session, June 14–15, Next Year.*

John smirks. "So, it's official—we're doing this every year?"

"You bet," Alicia says. "Because if we don't step back like this every twelve months, we'll slip into old habits. This keeps us aligned, focused, and accountable."

They have the vision. They have the direction. And now, they have the next step: Documenting what it means to become a Fully Aligned Student-Centered Organization.

As the team gathers their things and prepares to leave, Alicia looks out the window at the summer sun setting over the trees.

This is the work that matters.

And this time, it won't disappear when the next crisis comes along.

CORE MOTIVATION AND CORE VALUES

9

Alicia sits in her office, staring at the unopened email on her laptop. The cursor blinks, waiting.

Once news of Sheila's retirement got out, the district HR director was inundated with applications for the open position. She narrowed the list down to the top five and was ready for Alicia's input. Alicia steels herself as she opens the email, not wanting to face the possibility of what she might see. Sure enough, her worst fear is realized. At the top of the list is a name she knows all too well: John Anderson. Her eye-roller.

The assessment is that John had the education and experience to do the job of principal. He was Sheila's assistant principal for several years and knows every aspect of the high school—staff, students, and facilities—well. What was left unwritten was the fact that he did only the bare minimum that was required by his position; he didn't volunteer for extra duties; he refused any continuing education other than what was required to keep his licensure up to date.

And worst of all, John's habitual pushing back of any new initiatives had become exhausting.

"I know this is not what you wanted to see this morning," the email reads, "but on paper, he is the best fit for the position. Let me know if you need to talk things through."

Alicia closes the email and picks up her phone. She does need to talk things through, but not with HR. *Can you meet for coffee in the morning? Or hot chocolate?* she types. With a heavy sigh, she hits send.

THE RIGHT SEAT

The next morning, Alicia finds a quiet seat in the same coffee shop where she and Marcus had their first FASCO meeting. She recalls her initial hesitation and just as easily recalls the pounding headaches that marked the months leading up to her decision to dive into a new chapter. *How could I have ever doubted something that has literally saved my career?* She chuckles to herself.

She recalls the key points of the conversation she and Marcus had about making sure the right person is in the right role: Are they **a**ligned, **c**ommitted, and **e**quipped? The ACE acronym is easy to remember, and actually pretty easy to apply to this situation she faces. John is certainly equipped, but his lack of alignment and commitment is troubling. It is her job, Marcus instructed, to try to help John figure out why this is true. To have a hard discussion about what the issues are and whether or not they are solvable.

"This is where clarity becomes kindness," Marcus told her.

She sees John enter the shop before he notices her. His face is etched with a strange combination of fear and anticipation. And layered in all that is something Alicia can't quite put her finger on? *Is that sadness?*

"Morning, boss," he says, plopping down on the seat across from her, fingers nervously drumming the table between them.

Focus, she thinks as the barista serves their drinks. Marcus's words echo in her mind: "Get curious, not critical."

"Hi, John. Thank you for meeting me here this morning. I know it's not my usual MO, but I figured it might be good to get out of the office for a change." She takes a sip of coffee as John's agitation increases.

"Let me just say first of all that we haven't made a decision about Sheila's replacement yet," she says, reading his reaction. *Is that relief?* "I'd like to ask you to be completely honest with me today, John. Do you really want this job? Because it feels like you are just going through the motions, doing something that you're expected to do without any real buy-in or enthusiasm. Am I reading that right?"

John's facade seems to crumble. "Yeah, I guess that may be what is happening."

Alicia realizes he's becoming more emotional than he's comfortable with, so she gives him a beat to recover before asking, "Can you tell me what's going on?"

"My parents were small-town teachers," he begins, "and we always struggled financially growing up. Between raising us kids and working odd jobs to make ends meet, they never got around to furthering their education. Back then, you didn't just take out a loan to get a master's degree."

Alicia nods, remembering that her loan payment is due soon.

"School was always easy for me. I earned scholarship after scholarship—both academic and sports—so there was the expectation that I would pursue higher education. That I'd climb the ladder of school administration and make enough money so that life wasn't a constant struggle." He takes a sip of his coffee. "It was their dream for me."

"But it's not your dream, is it? You are obviously not happy in your current position. Why do you suppose that is?" Alicia asks, sensing they are nearing the heart of the issue.

"I really wanted to be a coach," he says.

INCREASING CLARITY WITH METHODS

Alicia waves and calls out greetings to her staff as she makes her way to her office. She feels like a hundred-pound weight has been lifted after her conversation with John. They agreed that he should withdraw his name from the running for Sheila's position and start putting out feelers for a more sports-centered opening. Whether he remains in her district or not, she feels like they reached a good solution.

She decides to tap into all the caffeine and good juju by starting to compile the book she had promised at the planning retreat. As Marcus explained, recording and simplifying key systems and processes with consistent **Methods** will hold the whole FASCO process together. These documented, repeatable ways of tracking things that matter become another check to ensure the student-first focus remains central.

Sitting down at her desk, she begins typing: *Becoming a Fully Aligned Student-Centered Organization.* It's tremendously exciting to consider that this book will serve as a road map for every staff member in the district. Before writing one word, she looks back on her notes from Marcus: *This should not be another lengthy strategic plan that gets shelved and forgotten. It needs to be simple, clear, and actionable.*

She takes a deep breath as the first line appears on her screen: Step 1: Identifying Our Core Values.

THE POWER OF CORE VALUES

At their next leadership meeting, Alicia stands at the white-board. "Before we finalize this book, we need to get something nailed down, and that is our Core Values."

Dan raises an eyebrow. "Didn't we already do that years ago? I remember a mission statement and some poster hanging in the district office."

"That's different," Alicia says. "A mission statement is what we strive for. Core Values are the principles that guide our daily actions and decisions. They're short, memorable, and something that students, staff, and the community can rally around."

She pauses. "And most importantly, they'll become the foundation for how we measure who belongs in our district. They'll be a part of hiring, evaluating, and coaching our team. They'll also help us navigate tough decisions when priorities compete."

Alicia can see John taking good notes as she continues. First, she pulls up a slide with examples from other organizations:

- Disney: Safety, Courtesy, Show, Efficiency
- Google: Focus on the user, Fast is better than slow, You can be serious without a suit
- Duke University: Respect, Trust, Inclusion, Discovery and Excellence

"These aren't paragraphs," Alicia says. "They're memorable, simple, and actionable."

Pam leans forward. "So, if we do this right, our Core Values will be more than words on a page—they'll be guideposts we actually use to lead?"

"Exactly," Alicia says and nods. "And if we want every layer of the Accountability Circle to be aligned—students, teachers, site staff, district staff, and the board—then we need Core Values that actually mean something."

THE CORE VALUES EXERCISE

Alicia hands out sticky notes. "We're going to do a simple exercise. Three rounds. No overthinking."

Round 1: The Gut Check
"Write down five to ten words or short phrases that represent the best of who we are when we're at our strongest. What do we want our students, staff, and community to see in us every day?"

The room goes quiet as people start writing. After a few minutes, they start placing their notes on the board. Words like the following:

• Integrity	• Student-First
• Accountability	• Excellence
• Growth	• Equity
• Compassion	• Innovation

Round 2: The Reality Check
When the last sticky note has been attached to the board, Alicia continues. "Now, take a hard look at this list and ask yourself: Would this pass the t-shirt test?"

Pam tilts her head. "The t-shirt test?"

"Yes," Alicia smiles. "Imagine a teacher, a student, or a parent walking around with this word or phrase on their shirt. Would it feel real, or would it feel like corporate fluff?"

A few chuckles ripple through the room as people start crossing out words that feel too generic or cliché.

New sticky notes start replacing the old ones:

- Be the Change
- You Belong Here

- Listen. Care.
  Follow-Through.

Round 3: The Commitment Check

"Final round," Alicia says. "Now, ask yourself: Would we actually make hiring and leadership decisions based on these? If someone wasn't living these values, would we call it out?"

A hush falls over the room. Alicia notices a few furtive glances sent John's way, but he seems oblivious as he seems deep in thought.

Then the real work begins. Some words disappear. Others get reworded.

Finally, the board settles into three Core Values:

✓ **Be the Change**—We don't wait for someone else to fix things. We lead.
✓ **You Belong Here**—Every student, staff member, and family should feel seen and valued.
✓ **Listen. Care. Follow-Through.**—Because great leadership starts with great relationships.

Alicia steps back and smiles. "These aren't just words. They're our standard—for how we work, how we lead, and who we hire."

Sheila, who has been quiet for most of the session, finally speaks. "I wish we had done this years ago."

Alicia nods. "So do I."

EMBEDDING CORE VALUES INTO FASCO

As the team regroups, Alicia updates their draft of the book.

Step 1: Core Values

Core Values are the foundation of a Fully Aligned Student-Centered Organization. They help us:

1. Hire the right people. Every new team member must align with our values.
2. Make tough decisions. When priorities compete, values help us choose the right path.
3. Build a lasting culture. These values aren't a poster. They're who we are—every day.

Our Core Values:

- ✓ **Be the Change**
- ✓ **You Belong Here**
- ✓ **Listen. Care. Follow-Through.**

ROLLING OUT THE FASCO GUIDE

With the first chapter of **Becoming a Fully Aligned Student-Centered Organization** complete, the team is energized. Over the next few weeks, they'll build out the rest—introducing the Accountability Circle, Vitals, Later List, and Rocks as essential tools for every staff member.

But one thing is clear: This isn't just another handbook.

This is how they will ensure that every student, teacher, and staff member is aligned, supported, and empowered.

And for the first time in her career, Alicia feels certain: this work will last.

NEW BEGINNINGS  10

Alicia stands on the back porch, a warm summer breeze drifting through the trees. The house is quiet, except for the occasional giggle from Logan and Olive inside, finishing up their last summer night of freedom. The first day of school outfits have been selected, lunches packed, and tablets are charging on the kitchen counter. She sips her tea and watches the fireflies dance in the yard, her mind replaying the past year like a highlight reel.

The late nights. The tough conversations. The moments of doubt.

But also—the breakthroughs. The clarity. The feeling that, for the first time, the work was being defined as more than simply keeping the district running. She and her team were building something visionary. Something that would last. And all the while, she still has time to take a break on the back porch.

Against her better judgment, Alicia had tucked her phone in her pocket on the way out the door. The night before school starts, she needs to be a hundred percent present in case of emergency. She jumps as it rings. Pam's ringtone. Oh no. She takes a deep breath. *Here we go.*

"Hey, Pam, what's up?"

"Alicia, I'm sorry to bother you this late, but I wanted you to know that I'm so excited about tomorrow. It's really happening. People are already starting to use the FASCO language. It's like we've discovered the Rosetta stone, and everyone is finally speaking the same language: Vitals, Later List, Rocks—all of it. This year is going to be the best, and I wanted to say thank you. Without you taking the risk of putting these new things in place, we would all be dreading what's to come. Now, we're just thrilled to get going. We might even make it without Sheila."

Alicia laughs. "That's probably going too far, but I get your point. It was so nice of you to call and give me this good report. I have to admit, when the phone rings, I'm usually expecting there to be a problem on the other end."

"No problems here. Only happy thoughts. See you in the morning."

NEW TERRITORY

Luis steps outside, throwing a blanket over Alicia's shoulders. "You OK? I thought I heard your phone ring."

"You did, but it wasn't a crisis. It was just one of my teammates gushing over the FASCO system and thanking me for taking the risk to implement it."

"Wow," he says, "that's new."

She nods, smiling. "And I've been thinking."

"Uh-oh." He grins.

She shakes a finger at him. "Don't worry, it's nothing bad like a new house project. I've been thinking about how different this year feels. Normally, I'd be bracing for impact. You remember those days: waiting for the first crisis, already feeling behind before the year even starts. The headaches. But now? It's the first time in a long time that I feel, well, ready."

Luis leans back against the railing, shoving his hands in his pockets. "That's really new."

Alicia chuckles. "I know. But it's true. We have a system now. The team knows where we're going. We're not scrambling anymore. People are really starting to use FASCO without having to be prompted. It's already making an impact. Honestly, this call from Pam is just the confirmation I needed to hear to believe it was really happening. This is real."

Suddenly, her phone buzzes with a text from Marcus: *Hey Alicia! I just got an application from John Anderson for our open athletic director position. He lists you as a reference. Thoughts?*

She smiles, typing a reply: *I think he'd be a great fit.*

A NEW CALLING

A year ago, Alicia was drowning. The weight of the district, the expectations, the feeling that every problem was hers to solve—it was suffocating.

Now, the district is something bigger than her. With courage and a lot of hard work, her team developed it into a Fully Aligned Student-Centered Organization, FASCO. The far-out idea that Marcus pitched to her in that deafening gymnasium, what seems like a lifetime ago, was no longer an idea on paper. It was tangible. She and her team were proof.

The Accountability Circle helped them understand their role in making students successful. That original organization model had made every district employee take a hard look at how they affect their students' quality of life.

Vitals kept them focused on what mattered most. Culling out the unnecessary data created an atmosphere where leading indicators were given primary focus. It was already making a difference in outcomes.

The Later List gave them permission to prioritize. Although coming to a consensus on what is most important created some conflict on the front end, the result was a clutter-free system that was key to full alignment.

Rocks ensured they made real progress every ninety days. More than a powerful visual reminder, Rocks locked in quarterly priorities that directly served their vision.

Vision gave them a path to follow; it was what anchored them to student success.

Methods brought everything together. And now, every new staff member would have a guide—a simple book to bring them into the culture and help them understand how things worked. Their success was poised to spread throughout the whole district. What an accomplishment!

Alicia glances at a printed proof of *Becoming a Fully Aligned Student-Centered Organization* sitting on the patio table. She runs her hand across the cover, feeling a deep sense of pride.

This wasn't just for her district anymore. This was something others could use, too.

Luis watches her for a moment. "Your team isn't the only thing that's been changing. You've been different these past few months."

"How so?" she asks.

"You're not just leading the district anymore. You're thinking bigger. It's like you've already got one foot in something new."

Alicia exhales. *He's not wrong.*

She loves the work they've done in the district, but a new thought has been pulling at her. What if other districts could do this, too? What if she could help them?

Marcus had done that for her. Now, maybe it was her turn.

She looks at Luis. "I think I'm ready for the next phase."

"And what's that?"

"I want to help other districts embrace FASCO. What if I could mentor other superintendents and leadership teams—help them create something sustainable, something that actually works for their students, staff, and community? I would really love to explore becoming a FASCO coach."

Luis nods, unsurprised. "So, not slowing down anytime soon, huh?"

Alicia laughs. "Nope. But at least now I know I don't have to do it alone."

She looks out over the yard, at the fireflies blinking against the night sky. For the first time in a long time, she isn't consumed with thoughts of simply making it through another school year. She's thinking about what's next. For her district, her team, and herself.

And she's ready.

PART 2

PUTTING THE TOOLS TO WORK

Now that you've seen the tools of a Fully Aligned Student-Centered Organization (FASCO) in action through Alicia's story, it's time to step behind the curtain. Part 2 is where we shift from storytelling to system building, where the real work begins. In this section, you'll learn how to implement each of the six tools introduced in Part 1 with clarity, structure, and confidence.

These tools aren't theoretical. They were designed by and for school and district leaders who needed something practical—something that would bring focus to the chaos, alignment to the team, and results to the students. Each part of the FASCO system exists because a problem existed first. These tools solve for things like blurred responsibilities, disconnected data, competing initiatives, unclear long-term direction, and leadership burnout.

The following pages were built to help you take action. You can work through Part 2 in order or jump to the section that addresses your most urgent challenge. Every chapter includes a deep explanation of the tool, guidance on how to roll it out with your team, and templates or sample language to support implementation. You will find that adopting the FASCO system is more than just grasping at another administration model. Here, your team will begin to accomplish things that matter, together, with structure.

Some leaders will choose to implement all six tools as a full FASCO system. Others will start with just one—often the Accountability Circle—and build momentum from there. The pace is up to you. What matters most is that each tool becomes part of your leadership rhythm, not just another professional development idea that fades after the next crisis hits.

As you work through this section, you'll notice that every tool is designed to help you keep students at the center, and every adult role is aligned in support of that mission. That's the power of FASCO. These aren't standalone strategies. When used together, they create a leadership system that outlives any one person and improves all aspects of your district or school over time.

So take a breath, clear some space, and get ready. You've seen what these tools can do in a fictional narrative. Now let's shape them into your reality.

THE ACCOUNTABILITY CIRCLE

The Accountability Circle is a unique organizational structure designed to reframe how we view leadership and responsibility within a school system. The circle's purpose is simple yet powerful: to keep students at the center of every decision, every structure, and every action.

Most school systems default to a top-down hierarchy that unintentionally disconnects leadership from the day-to-day experiences of students. The Accountability Circle flips that mindset. Instead of placing the school board or superintendent at the top, we place students at the center and then build outwards in layers of support.

LAYERS OF THE CIRCLE

Each layer of the Accountability Circle plays a critical role in helping students grow and thrive. The closer a layer is to the student, the more direct its impact and the more support it requires from the outer layers. Let's start at the center:

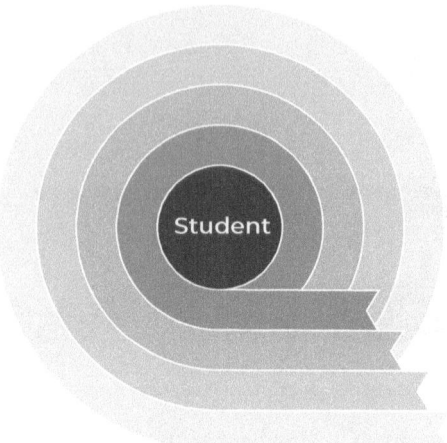

Center: The Student

Everything begins here. The singular goal of a school system—to equip young people for a productive future—demands a singular model for administration. Under FASCO, students are not the "end users," rather, they are the sole reason the organization exists. All roles, structures, and initiatives must ultimately serve student growth, well-being, and success. Where traditional models miss the mark is when the focus is on the administration or even the teachers. If we say we are there primarily to serve students, putting them in the center of all our efforts is a common-sense approach to managing a school system.

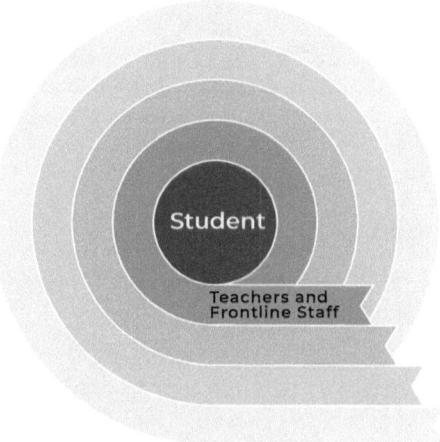

First Layer: Teachers and Frontline Staff

This crucial layer includes classroom teachers, instructional aides, paraprofessionals, bus drivers, cafeteria workers, and any other staff who interact with students on a daily basis. Their job is to create meaningful, engaging, and safe learning environments. Their effectiveness depends on having the time, training, and trust to do the work well. Not surprisingly, growth in this layer has the most immediate impact on students.

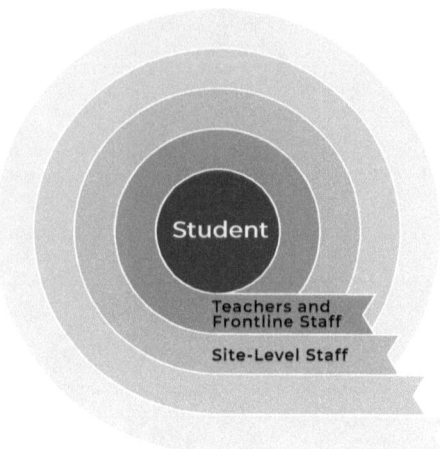

Second Layer: Site-Level Staff

This layer provides the leadership and environment that enables teachers and frontline staff (e.g., principals, assistant principals, counselors, food service staff) to thrive. Activities and initiatives within this layer act as a buffer, removing distractions and solving problems so that teachers can focus on students. For example, principals are tasked with creating school-wide clarity and consistency. Counselors, deans, and even the kitchen crew build supportive systems for students and families.

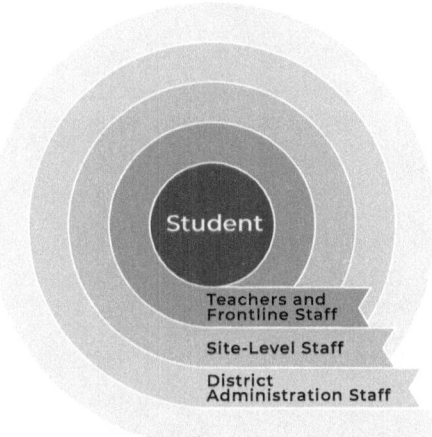

Third Layer: District Administration Staff

This layer exists to support site teams so that they, in turn, can support teachers and students. It is intentionally broken into key areas of expertise:

- Instructional: Curriculum leaders, instructional coaches, assessment teams, and PD facilitators who ensure teaching and learning are effective and equitable.
- Operations: Facilities, transportation, nutrition services, and logistics teams that make the daily operations of schools possible.
- Support Services: HR, finance, IT, and communications—often behind-the-scenes, but critical in creating a responsive, well-functioning system.

Important Reminder: No layer can grow if the layers that support it are stagnant or dysfunctional. Growth must be systemic. If teachers are struggling, we don't just "train them better," we examine whether their site staff and district supports are also evolving.

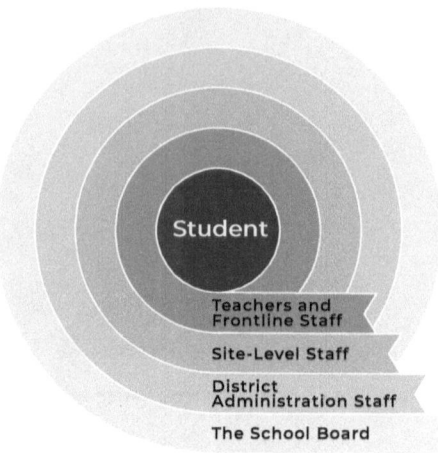

Fourth Layer: The School Board

The outermost layer of the Accountability Circle is the school board. While not involved in daily operations, the board plays a pivotal role in enabling the growth of every other layer. First, it establishes direction by defining long-term goals, approving policies, and adopting district vision and values. The board also allocates resources by approving budgets and ensuring adequate support for strategic priorities. Finally, the board hires and evaluates the superintendent. This is its most direct influence on district leadership and direction.

The school board's effectiveness is measured not only by its intentions but also by how clearly it understands and supports the growth of each inner layer. If the board is misaligned, every other layer feels the impact.

EXERCISE:

DEFINING DISTRICT-LEVEL ROLES IN THE ACCOUNTABILITY CIRCLE

Please note: As the district leader, you will work through this exercise twice—once by yourself, and then again with your leadership team.

This part is important.

You must do this exercise on your own first before involving your team, not because you don't trust them, but for the following reasons:

- *It reveals your own thinking.* You need to see how clearly *you* understand your system before inviting others to weigh in.
- *It protects objectivity.* When you start with names or titles, people defend roles instead of discussing what's best for students.
- *It gives you a baseline.* Later, when you engage your leadership team (which we will walk through in the next section), you'll be able to compare your perspective to theirs.

You are designing a system that outlasts personalities. That's leadership.

This is not just an organizational chart exercise. It's a leadership clarity exercise. We are designing the system that will support every layer beneath it, and ultimately, help students thrive. Misaligned, every other layer feels the impact.

We begin near the outside of the Accountability Circle at the district-level circle and move inward.

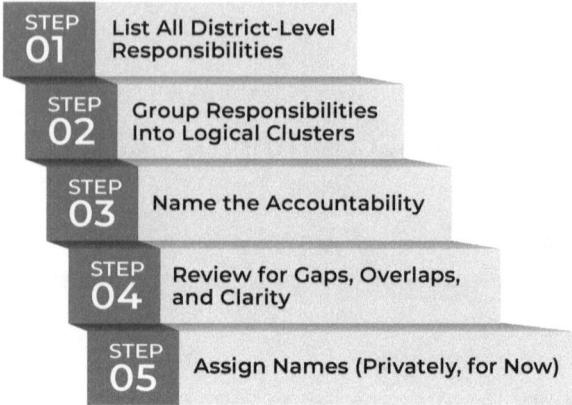

STEP
01 — List All District-Level Responsibilities

STEP
02 — Group Responsibilities Into Logical Clusters

STEP
03 — Name the Accountability

STEP
04 — Review for Gaps, Overlaps, and Clarity

STEP
05 — Assign Names (Privately, for Now)

Step 1: List All District-Level Responsibilities (No Titles Yet)

Start by thinking through everything your district is responsible for at the central office level across instructional, operations, and support services. The list should be long. Don't filter yet.

Think across these categories:

- Student learning
- Instructional support
- Facilities, transportation, and meals
- Budget and finance
- HR and staffing
- IT and systems
- Family and community engagement
- Compliance and risk management

Example items:

- Math curriculum alignment
- Budget development and forecasting
- School safety protocols
- Onboarding and retention of staff

- Transportation route planning
- State and federal reporting compliance
- Substitute coverage process
- Assessment platform support
- Internal communications
- Special education IEP compliance
- Strategic plan monitoring
- High school graduation tracking
- Technology device refresh cycle
- Bilingual services coordination
- Facility repairs and maintenance
- Social media and district website
- Hiring and credentialing processes

Tip: Ask your cabinet or direct reports to submit their task list. You'll often find two hundred-plus items when you combine them.

Step 2: Group Responsibilities Into Logical Clusters
Now step back. Begin organizing the responsibilities into **natural groupings** of three to five items. Each group should reflect a **distinct area of accountability** that could reasonably be owned by one person.

You're not looking for job descriptions yet. You're uncovering the structure your system actually needs.

Example groupings:

- Instructional Assessment and Data
  - Assessment platform oversight
  - State testing coordination
  - Data dashboards
  - School-level data coaching

- Human Resources Operations
  - Hiring and credentialing
  - Employee onboarding
  - Substitute coordination
  - Employee evaluations
- Student Services
  - Special education support
  - Section 504 and IEP compliance
  - Bilingual programs
  - MTSS framework and systems

Tip: If you find a group has only one or two items, it may be a sub-responsibility. If a group has seven or more, it may need to be broken apart or better defined.

Step 3: Name the Accountability (Still No People Assigned Yet)
Throughout this process, you may struggle to categorize responsibilities without assigning people, at least in your head. Resist that urge for just a little bit longer. Once you've created these groups that make logical sense together, give each one a **functional accountability name**.

Examples:

- Elementary Curriculum
- Instructional Technology
- Financial Planning and Compliance
- Facility Operations
- Talent Acquisition and Retention

This will later become the "role" within your Accountability Circle, but don't assign names yet.

Step 4: Review for Gaps, Overlaps, and Clarity

Closely examine the following areas:

- Gaps: Is any essential function missing?
- Overlaps: Are multiple groups doing similar work?
- Clarity: Are any roles too vague to hold someone accountable? If it's too vague to measure progress or define success, it's not yet a clear accountability item.

No matter how things "have always been done," you should be able to discern where improvements can be made. This is what it's all about.

Step 5: Assign Names (Privately, for Now)

Only after completing Steps 1 through 4, place one name next to each accountability. Resist the urge to jump ahead to this step.

- Each accountability can only have **one owner**.
- A person can own **more than one accountability** (especially in smaller districts), but no accountability should be shared.
- Don't worry if the names don't match your current org chart. This process is meant to **reveal the structure you need**, not justify the structure you have.

ENGAGING YOUR LEADERSHIP TEAM

Once you've done the initial work of mapping the district-level accountabilities on your own, the next step is to engage your leadership team. This part builds alignment and buy-in, ensuring your structure reflects reality from multiple perspectives.

Reminder: You don't need a perfect structure before involving others. You only need a thoughtful draft and a willingness to listen.

Why bring in the leadership team? When leaders are invited into the process of defining accountability rather than being handed a new chart, a few powerful things happen:

- They see how their work connects to the student-centered mission.
- They feel ownership over the structure, not just compliance.
- You uncover blind spots or duplications that may not have been visible before.
- You shift from *person-driven leadership* to *purpose-driven leadership*.

This is absolutely a process you can facilitate yourself. But depending on the size of your district or the dynamics of your team, it is also a great moment to bring in a certified FASCO trained coach to support the process. Our coaches are carefully vetted and trained professionals with educational leadership experience. In addition to being experts in the FASCO system, they are adept facilitators with proven abilities to help shift your culture and implement meaningful change.

A coach can help by:

- Smoothing out hard conversations with neutrality
- Keeping the group focused on accountability, not personalities
- Providing templates and examples from other districts

- Helping translate this process into a clear, sustainable operating structure

If this is your first time working through the Accountability Circle, a coach can dramatically reduce the friction and accelerate clarity.

HOW TO FACILITATE THE LEADERSHIP TEAM EXERCISE

First, set the tone. Some team members may be understandably concerned about a meeting involving district or school roles. Reassure them that you have no intention of going after anyone's job or pet project. You are simply moving to create a structure that benefits students above all else.

Start the session with a clear message: "Today, we are not focusing on job titles or evaluations. We are starting to build a student-centered system that supports clarity, growth, and better outcomes. We're going to define what needs to be done, then make sure it's getting done, and only then assign ownership."

Next, review the process. Walk the team through the steps you have already worked through without projecting your results on the group:

- List all responsibilities without naming names
- Group them into logical buckets
- Name each bucket as an accountability
- Then and only then assign one owner

Then compare your draft with the group's outcomes. If you've already done the exercise solo, you have a draft. Share it only after the team goes through the exercise themselves. This allows for shared discovery and transparency. It also promotes healthy discussion. The team will appreciate your extensive preparation and sense your complete faith in the process.

While sharing your draft, take the opportunity to compare diverging ideas and consolidate similar thoughts.

Next, clarify ownership. Use sticky notes, a whiteboard, or digital collaboration tools to assign one name per accountability.

Don't confuse collaboration with ownership. Many people may be involved in a responsibility, but only one person is accountable.

Finally, capture the final structure. After healthy debate and adjustments, tie up your district-level Accountability Circle. This should include role names by accountability (e.g., "secondary curriculum," not "John") with one owner per role. Make sure there is a clear understanding across the team by taking questions.

By the end of this process, your leadership team should have a shared understanding of what district-level work needs to be owned; clarity on who owns what; and a structure that aligns with your mission and reduces confusion.

And a key outcome should be the understanding that a culture of accountability starts with purpose—not people.

DO THEY ACE THE ROLE?

Once you've defined the duties within the Accountability Circle, it's time to assess whether the right person is in the right seat. This is at the same time the most rewarding and most difficult step of the process.

As we saw in our fable, once Alicia took the time to discover why her vice principal had such an attitude problem, better outcomes were in store for both of them. No matter how skilled she was at motivating her team, she knew John would never be a true contributing member in a job he felt pressured by others to fill.

Alicia used the ACE Test—a quick and powerful way to determine role fit. In the ACE model, A stands for *aligned*; C stands for *committed*; and E stands for *equipped*. Here are some specific questions to ask yourself and your employees about the seats they currently occupy. Don't overthink these questions. Stick with a simple yes or no as you answer. The most honest result will come from your instinctive reactions.

Aligned

Do they understand and believe in the purpose of the role?

- The team member sees how the work contributes to student success. You frequently hear about their satisfaction in being a key part of students' lives.
- They align with the mission, values, and outcomes expected. This is reflected in consistent completion of assigned tasks and going the extra mile.
- They bring clarity and perspective to the position. Happy to answer questions, they serve as an ambassador of the system and their place in it.

Committed

Do they genuinely want the responsibility and own the outcomes?

- These team members take initiative and don't need to be pushed. They may not always raise their hands for extra duties, but they aren't averse to new challenges.

- They are engaged and motivated by the work itself. In addition, they are quick to acknowledge their part in any situations that don't go as intended.
- They bring energy and presence to the role. Those in the right seat can't help but share their positivity and enthusiasm.

Equipped

Do they have the skills, time, and support to lead this area well?

- They are capable of executing the work consistently. This is a measurable outcome. Take a look at the concrete evidence of a job well done.
- They have the resources, systems, and support needed to succeed. If there are gaps here, it's up to you to fill them in or point the way to someone who can.
- They aren't overloaded or out of their depth. If they are, again, it's up to you to provide educational resources, mentoring, or advice on possibly changing roles.

Ask yourself (or your team): Do they ACE the role? Are they aligned, committed, and equipped? If any one of the three is missing, the role—and the students it ultimately serves—will suffer. You may want to start with yourself.

WHEN SOMEONE DOESN'T ACE THE ROLE
(OR DOESN'T HAVE A ROLE AT ALL)

This is the moment every leader dreads, and also the moment that separates real leadership from simple management. After you've defined your Accountability Circle and used the ACE Framework to assess role fit, you may find that:

- Someone doesn't ACE the role they're in.
- Someone is in a role that no longer fits any real accountability.
- Someone is in a role that overlaps too heavily with someone else's.

If you discover any of those situations, it's just a matter of time before this role misalignment will cause problems. It's up to you to take corrective action. As Marcus taught Alicia, this is where clarity becomes kindness.

Don't panic. These results are normal. You are not doing something wrong. This is simply what happens when we design roles around people instead of starting with what students and systems need.

Now that you've reversed that process—starting with clarity and purpose—you're just seeing your organization clearly for the first time.

Organizational development consultant Peter Block is credited with saying, "Structure reveals truth. Truth invites action." Your first action is contemplation.

Get curious, not critical.
Ask yourself which of the three ACE elements is missing. There may be more than one.

Is it a clarity issue (not aligned)? A motivation issue (not committed)? A bandwidth or support issue (not equipped)? John had the best principal in the district and a stellar resume. His issues were more focused on disparities in alignment and motivation.

Have a one-on-one conversation.

Your goal is not to remove someone. It's to get them and your system back into alignment. Don't enter the dialogue with a solution in mind. Your first job is to get to the root of the problem.

Share what you're seeing, invite them to reflect, and explore what could change to get back to ACE.

Use the Later List (chapter 13).

Not all decisions need to happen immediately. As we saw with Alicia and John, they came to an agreement that he would begin exploring other positions. Alicia did not pressure him to resign.

If you're unsure where someone fits, place their role discussion on the Later List so it stays visible without forcing a reactive decision.

Document as you go.

Email a brief recap of your discussion to the team member and copy your HR director. This ensures you both heard the same things and also serves as a nonthreatening way to protect yourself against complaints.

Keep notes on any roles, gaps, or adjustments that may need to be revisited at your next quarterly planning session.

Once your team is fully aligned around the FASCO model, you'll introduce a new practice: the Quarterly ACE Analysis. Change is inevitable. Circumstances change, people change, funding changes, and you must be ready to pivot.

The Quarterly ACE Analysis is a one-on-one tool used by leaders with their direct reports once per quarter to answer one powerful question: Do they ACE the role they're in right now?

The analysis is part reflection, part feedback, and part strategic review. It ensures that no one drifts too far off course without support or conversation. This is just one of many tools available on the FASCO website's Alignment Hub.

CONCLUSION

Once you've established the Accountability Circle that works best for your district, you will notice a shift. Where there was once a feeling of fragmentation, you will begin to see cohesiveness. Where there was previously a stack of projects left undone due to accountability issues, you will see progress. And, best of all, where you may have been questioning your ability to serve students and staff well, you will have a clear picture of successes and areas for improvement.

With that system of responsibilities firmly in place, you have the framework set to add another key FASCO tool. This next essential strategy will help cut through the noise and complexity that distracts you and your team from progress toward student success. It's time to take the pulse of your district and focus on what matters most. It's time to take your Vitals.

VITALS: EVERY ROLE OWNS A NUMBER

In a Fully Aligned Student-Centered Organization, clarity drives performance. After establishing the Accountability Circle, the next step in alignment is to focus on data that matters. Numbers that keep you moving forward. That's what Vitals are: the minimum set of key metrics that indicate if your system is healthy and heading in the right direction. Clear, outcome-focused metrics for which one person—just one—is held accountable.

As Marcus explained to Alicia in Part 1, when you visit the doctor, they check a few things—blood pressure, temperature, pulse—to determine if your essential systems are working properly. They don't need your cholesterol levels and genetic markers if you are being treated for the flu.

The same principle applies to your school system. With Vitals, you're not trying to track everything. You're monitoring only the most important things; the ones that truly matter and can trigger action.

For example, looking at your desired graduation rates, what levers are there in your organization that contribute to that outcome? Attendance rates? Third-grade reading proficiency? Daily schedule? The goal is to reverse engineer your goals and focus on the metrics that play into them. When you pinpoint the things that happen in your system day after day and week after week, it helps create a repeatable technique that will result in the student success you are after.

NOT JUST ANY DATA

Vitals are not a long spreadsheet of Key Performance Indicators (KPIs), compliance checklists, or dashboard for the sake of reporting.

Vitals are your district's most important measurements; the data that shows if your board, team, school, or system is thriving. With Vitals, if something is missing the mark, it quickly becomes apparent, and you can take corrective action. You don't wait for the quarterly meeting or even the annual retreat to identify any adjustments that may need to be made. Weekly, or even daily, reporting creates an environment where change can happen quickly, averting potential crises and ensuring the outcome you're working toward.

To get started thinking along these lines, let's look at some potential examples of Vitals sorted by role type.

Instructional Roles

- Percentage of students at or above benchmark this week
- Teacher coaching sessions completed this week
- Number of PLCs led or attended
- Percentage of classrooms visited with feedback logged

Operations Roles

- Percentage of buses on time this week
- Number of open maintenance work orders over five days

- Percentage of kitchen inspections passed
- Staff coverage ratio (subs/day)

Support Services

- Time to fill open positions
- Percentage of payroll errors corrected within forty-eight hours
- Percentage of tech tickets closed within three business days
- Weekly engagement rates on internal comms

Principals/Site Leader

- Weekly student attendance (leading version)
- Percentage of staff observed and given feedback this week
- Number of family contacts made by office staff
- Percentage of on-track academic check-ins completed

School Board

- Meeting attendance rates
- Community feedback
- Funding tracking
- Local and federal law compliance

You may have noticed that each role in our examples is not assigned a plethora of data points to track. Rather, we follow what we call FASCO's Rule of Vitals:

| Every role in your Accountability Circle™ must own a number | Maximum of 5 Vitals and Minimum of 1 Vital | Ideal: As few as possible, without losing sight of the role's impact |

HOW TO CHOOSE THE RIGHT VITALS

The process of choosing your Vitals begins with a few simple questions. Start by contemplating each role in your Accountability Circle:

- What outcome is this role accountable for?
- What number would tell us in real time if we're on track or off track?
- What's the most *leading indicator* we can measure?

A leading indicator, or leading Vital, is a key phrase in this process. You don't want to wait until the semester is over to discover something is broken. Rather, you want to see any misdirection in time to change the outcome. Your students don't get a do-over for the year once you discover a problem that kept them from succeeding.

The solution? Concentrate on the data that can make all the difference in what's to come. The Leading Vitals can tell us what's about to happen before it actually does. Far from mystical, this proven economic principle exposes subtle changes in data in time to avert disastrous results.

For example:

Lagging Indicator	Leading Vital (Real-Time)
Semester attendance rate	Percentage of students who missed two-plus days this week
End-of-year reading proficiency	Percentage of students below benchmark on this week's check-in
Annual staff turnover rate	Percentage of staff flagged as "disconnected" in weekly check-ins
Discipline referrals per semester	Number of major incidents this week per school

The more real-time and actionable the Vital, the more powerful it becomes.

EXERCISE:

IMPLEMENTING VITALS ACROSS YOUR TEAM

This may be one of the most challenging exercises you do while incorporating the FASCO system, but with these step-by-step actions you'll be amazed at how much fog will dissipate by the time you are finished. Calling on a certified FASCO coach for this part of the process is also highly recommended. Their specialized training, along with their knowledge of how other districts have zeroed in on Vitals, will put you and your team at ease.

To pull everyone into this process most effectively, have a copy of your Accountability Circle roles close at hand. Before diving in, do a brief review of leading indicators versus lagging indicators and give a few examples. Vitals will make the biggest impact if you focus on metrics that create positive outcomes rather than reporting on what has already happened. Also, it doesn't hurt to give another reminder that no one is going to lose their job because of what happens in the meeting.

Have a whiteboard and piles of sticky notes handy, and dive in.

First, define the accountability. You can't assign a Vital without clarity on what the role is meant to achieve. Refer back to your Accountability Circle roles. What are three or four primary responsibilities for each position?

Second, brainstorm potential metrics. Don't hold back! As we hear so often in the classroom, "No idea is a dumb idea." Embrace that here as you use whiteboards or sticky notes. List as many data points as possible, then cut ruthlessly. Ask, "If this number moved, for better or worse, would it impact students?" If the answer is no, it's not a Vital.

Third, prioritize leading indicators. Students are best served when leadership pivots mid-stream to avert a problem. Hindsight may be twenty-twenty, but it doesn't help when it's too late to change anything. Stay leading-indicator focused by asking: Can this data point be measured weekly or bi-weekly? Is it possible to be alerted to changes to this metric in time to be proactive? If the answer to one or both of those questions is yes, you have probably uncovered something to add to your Vitals list.

Finally, assign ownership. One person must own each Vital. They don't have to do all the work, but they are the point of accountability for that number. Encourage team members to volunteer to assist with others' Vitals, but when the next meeting comes around, the primary owner reports on and owns the results. What you will find is that when people start managing their own Vitals, they will be able to identify issues before having to be told to address them. When your team is collecting their own Vitals every week, they start managing themselves. Sounds great, doesn't it?

CONCLUSION

School leaders tell us that one of the hardest tasks they undertake is keeping track of countless data. Not only does the volume of traditional systems make it hard to spot trouble spots, but also, even when problems are identified, they tend to get lost in the day-to-day responsibilities of keeping a district on course. That's the beauty of FASCO Vitals. Every team member has clear responsibilities and a regular check-in process.

Once your Vitals are established, head over to the FASCO Alignment Hub to enter your team's results. Then watch as your dashboard tracks metrics; is what you are seeing a trend or an anomaly? Does a key metric need to be moved to another owner? This piece of the FASCO puzzle will help create a more aligned, forward-focused environment benefiting students and staff alike. It gives you a clear, ongoing pulse of what matters most.

But what about those things that, at least for the moment, are not Vitals? How do you keep from losing sight of important metrics that are not urgent? The next FASCO tool was designed to help with just that.

THE LATER LIST: PROTECT YOUR FOCUS

It happens to everyone: In the middle of the night, you are startled awake by the thought of something you forgot to take care of. Did you close the garage door? Put the garbage on the curb? Send out the agenda for tomorrow morning's meeting? Some things are trivial, but some are more impactful. In the daily grind of educational administration, you can't afford to lose sight of important tasks and goals.

You will never run out of issues to solve, but in a Fully Aligned Student-Centered Organization, they don't have to keep you up at night. The problem is, when everything is urgent, you may naturally solve some issues, but most of your energy will be spent spinning in circles. And while distractions may relentlessly dilute your attention and energy, you don't have to lose focus if you set up a system to track your lower-priority tasks.

This is where the FASCO Later List comes in. The Later List is a living tool that helps you and your team stay keyed in on what matters *now*, without losing track of what may matter *later*.

WHAT IS THE LATER LIST?

The Later List is a simple tool used to capture important but nonurgent issues. It protects your current focus by prioritizing when the timing is right to act. Through revisiting the list in a regular rhythm, nothing falls by the wayside.

The list is not a junk drawer, parking lot, or even a graveyard. It's a holding tank for future clarity. It is developed through a process to discern what should be a high priority and what should not.

Steve Jobs understood the importance of the Later List principle when he said, "Discipline is saying no to good ideas so you can say yes to the right ones."

Without a Later List, every "good idea" becomes a fire drill requiring the same exhausting level of urgency, whether it is warranted or not. Teams shift priorities weekly or sometimes even daily. Your best thinking is lost in sticky notes and side conversations. Team members are overcommunicating ideas and complaints when there is no one tasked with follow-up. In short, without a Later List, people feel overwhelmed, unclear, and reactive.

But once a Later List is put in place, some amazing things begin to happen. Every new idea has a home. Priorities are protected rather than fought over. Important conversations happen at the right time. The Later List give you the power to stop and ask yourself, "Do I really need to send that message right now?" Best of all, organizing nonurgent priorities teaches your team to pause and lead with intention.

HOW TO BUILD AND USE THE LATER LIST

While the Accountability Circle and Vitals require an initial face-to-face with stakeholders, creating a Later List can be done with a combination of nonverbal communication and meetings. Here's how to get started:

First, create a shared document. Organize a spreadsheet, slide, or whiteboard—whatever works best for your team. Use the key terms Now and Later as the list develops. Make a note that everyone can contribute, but only the leadership team can move items from column to column. Consider setting this up inside FASCO's Alignment Hub, so your Later List becomes a tracked, central source that's easy to revisit, reprioritize, and update over time—giving the leadership team a clear, living record of future priorities.

Second, add items as they arise. Any time something new comes up—in meetings, emails, hallway conversations—ask: "Is this a *Now*, or a *Later?*" If it's *Later*, log it with a brief description, the person who raised it, and any time sensitivity associated with the item.

Third, review the Later List weekly in your huddle. Your weekly huddle flow might look something like this:

- Review Vitals—What's off track?
- Progress on Rocks (more on Rocks in chapter 14)—What's moving forward?
- Check the Later List—Anything we need to pull to Now?

Only move something from *Later* to *Now* if it is more urgent or more impactful than your current top priorities, or if you are dropping or closing something else to make space.

The *Now* column is finite and must be protected, or the whole process will derail.

And finally, sort and group quarterly. At your Quarterly Planning Session, review items on the Later List and ask the following questions:

- What should become a top priority this quarter?
- What's no longer relevant?
- What needs to stay on the list?

With careful maintenance, the Later List protects focus while allowing new ideas to blossom.

Examples of Items That Belong on the Later List

Example Item	Why It Goes on the Later List
Redesign the report card system	Important, but not urgent this quarter
Launch a student podcast initiative	Great idea, but doesn't align with current Rocks
Revamp all lunch menus	Valid concern—needs research and timing
New PLC structure for secondary schools	Not ready yet—needs more input

THE DECISION-MAKING FILTER

When your team adds an item to the Later List, you don't want it to sit there indefinitely or, worse yet, get pulled forward too soon. You need a clear, shared way to evaluate each item so your team can act with focus, not emotion.

The FASCO system uses a two-question filter to do just that:

1. **Is it urgent?** *Does this need to be solved this week?*
   - Yes = time-sensitive, blocking progress, or has a deadline
   - No = can wait without major consequence
2. **Is it important?** *Is this a mission-critical issue?*
   - Yes = directly affects student outcomes, staff well-being, or strategic goals
   - No = helpful or interesting, but not essential

For every item added to the Later List, answer those two questions. Then place the item in one of four quadrants:

FASCO Urgency/Importance Quadrant

Importance ↓ / Urgency →	Urgent (Yes to "Is it urgent?")	Not Urgent (No to "Is it urgent?")
Important (Yes to "Is it important?")	Quadrant 1: Act Now Time-sensitive, blocking progress, mission-critical. Address this week.	Quadrant 2: Schedule Mission-critical but not time-sensitive. Plan and resource for completion without rushing.
Not Important (No to "Is it important?")	Quadrant 3: Delegate Needs to happen soon but not mission-critical— hand off to others.	Quadrant 4: Park/ Later List Nice-to-have ideas or improvements. Capture in Alignment Hub for future review.

Urgent	Important	What To Do
✔ Yes	✔ Yes	**Prioritize**—Move into this week's discussion or Next Steps
✖ No	✔ Yes	**Schedule or Scope**—Discuss in future planning (e.g., quarterly)
✔ Yes	✖ No	**Delegate or Triage**—Address with minimal time or redirect focus
✖ No	✖ No	**Park It**—Keep on the Later List, review again later

Later List Item Tracker (with Decision Filter)

Later List Item	Urgent	Important	Action	Notes
Redesign PD calendar	✖ No	✔ Yes	Scope for next quarter	Needs broader input
New school app	✔ Yes	✖ No	Delegate for research	Explore options
Transportation route changes	✔ Yes	✔ Yes	Prioritize and assign this week	Creating daily disruptions
Update playground equipment	✖ No	✖ No	Park it	Add to facilities review

EXERCISE:

FASCO WEEKLY HUDDLE AGENDA

Timeframe: 45–60 minutes

Cadence: Weekly

Purpose: Align, focus, follow through, and build a culture of accountability

The Weekly Huddle is the most important hour of your week as an educational administrator. This is where you get to connect with your team, experience the good and bad days together, and keep your vision for their success in clear view. With the FASCO system, your time is never wasted. Here's a sample agenda to keep your meetings flowing and productive:

Intro and Share Win of the Week (5 min)

Each team member shares one quick personal or professional highlight. This sets the tone for the meeting with connection and momentum.

Review Rocks and Vitals (10–15 min)

The team then reviews the most important metrics—the ones that show whether we're healthy and moving forward.
For each Rock and Vital:

- On Track/Off Track
- If Off Track: Brief note on why (no solving here)
- Add related items to the Later List if needed

Review Action Items from Previous Week (5–10 min)

Check whether all action items—especially those created by **CLEARed** issues (see below)—were completed.

Celebrate the wins and document the updated plan on uncompleted tasks. No blame, just follow-through.

Review the Later List (15–20 min)

Use the Urgent + Important Filter:

- Urgent? Does this need to be solved this week?
- Important? Is this mission-critical?

Choose from the following action steps:

- CLEAR it
- Park it
- One Yes = scope, schedule, or delegate

CLEAR It from the List (as needed)

The CLEAR Framework should be used to resolve items fully. It's important to note that all stakeholders for the issue you are trying to CLEAR must be present for this discussion. It should be done sequentially and thoroughly, and you may need to draw opinions out from the more reticent members of your team. These are discussions where true conflict may emerge in an organization, and those who can handle that in a productive manner are the ones who actually solve the issues. Work through each of these steps, with the important final note to make one person responsible for the action item:

C   Define the core issue (it may not be obvious)

L   Listen to input and stakeholders

E   Explore possible solutions

A   Agree on the best path (there will not always be consensus here)

R   Assign one responsible person

All CLEARed items result in an action due within seven days. Don't forget to document the agreed-upon outcome. Remind your team that even if they don't buy into the decisions made, you expect their support for the group's judgment. Don't underestimate the power the CLEAR Framework wields to help you move beyond the status quo in your organization.

Quite honestly, the CLEAR process may initially be difficult for your team. It frequently leads to side discussions and the temptation to veer away from the core issue. This is another instance where FASCO coaches can step in to help keep the team on task until they are comfortable CLEARing items on their own.

CLEAR
Framework Example

Define core issue: Funding has come through to increase high school counseling staff to respond to increasing mental health concerns.

Listen to input and stakeholders: Ensure all layers of the Accountability Circle are present and engaged.

Explore possible solutions: Determine number of counselors you are seeking, along with their academic qualifications and experience; ensure job descriptions and compensation packages are up to date.

Agree on the best path: Will you pull from part-time counselors in other buildings or districts? Move part-time employees to full-time? Advertise outside the district? Use a recruiting service?

Assign one responsible person: Name HR representative who will begin the hiring process.

Wrap-Up (5–7 min)

- Recap new action items and who owns them
- Shout-Outs (2 min): "Who deserves a thank-you or recognition this week?"
- Meeting Rating (1–10): "How valuable was this meeting today?" Invite comments on ratings of seven or below.

For every Later List item, be sure to document the next step, even if the next step is to do nothing at the current time. When this process is complete, you have accomplished something previously unthinkable: freed up space in your brain for taking on the truly important things this day holds.

CONCLUSION

Motivational speaker and author Molly Fletcher said, "Discipline isn't just about saying no. It's about knowing what to say yes to—and when." That's the essence of the Later List. Logically thinking through tasks and priorities with the help of your team, and then organizing them in a place they won't disappear from view, naturally clears the way for progress. The Later List function of the FASCO Alignment Hub is a tremendous tool to help free you up to say yes to what's most important. Along with a supportive community, you will find everything you need to keep your many responsibilities under control.

When you begin to clear out the clutter, those things of top importance naturally come into view. It's the next FASCO tool you can now see clearly: your Rocks.

THE POWER OF ROCKS TO PROPEL FORWARD MOTION

14

As we saw in Alicia's story, attempting to do everything yourself is a recipe for burnout. You can't do everything, but you *can* do the most important things, and that's what Rocks will help your team accomplish.

Rocks are a powerful FASCO tool that creates and maintains a list of your top priorities. This highlights the major initiatives your leadership team commits to for the next ninety days. Rocks bring urgency, focus, and alignment to the work that matters most, so you can make real progress instead of just treading water. With weekly review and quarterly reorganization, Rocks help create the focus that moves the organization forward.

THE LOGIC BEHIND ROCKS

We call our quarterly priorities Rocks for a reason, and it comes from a simple, powerful visual about how we spend our time and energy. One that Alicia shared with her team in Part 1.

Imagine you have an empty jar sitting on a table. Next to it, you have a pile of big rocks, a scoop of pebbles, a handful of sand, and a glass of water. The challenge is to fit all of it into the jar.

If you start by pouring in the water, then the sand, then the pebbles, by the time you try to add the big rocks, they simply won't fit. The jar is already full of all the small stuff.

But if you start by placing the big rocks in the jar first, then pour in the pebbles, then the sand, and finally the water, it all fits. Why? Because you prioritized the most important items first. Everything else, the normal questions, crises, and responsibilities of your day, can fill in around them in the most efficient manner possible.

That's exactly how we treat quarterly planning in a Fully Aligned Student-Centered Organization. The Rocks are your biggest priorities. They are the initiatives that will move your students, staff, and systems forward. And Rocks don't appear out of nowhere. They have to be put in the jar first. Otherwise, the distractions of the week-to-week—the pebbles and sand of daily operations—will crowd them out.

By naming them, committing to them, and checking on them weekly, you make sure your team is always focused on what matters most rather than what's making the most noise.

If your team is tuned into the regular cadence of a weekly meeting, none of the Rocks will come as a surprise. Everyone will be able to come to every meeting prepared to discuss next steps for each of your upcoming large projects. It may be a Vital that is missing the mark, or a role that needs increased support or definition. Whatever the issue, crafting your Rocks brings cohesiveness to the group and results for the district. Often, this process uncovers a root issue that can be solved once and for all, creating a solution that is system-driven rather than person-driven.

If there is something that needs to be fundamentally communicated, explained, and assimilated across an organization, then that something would be deemed a Rock.

Let's take the example of updating or reviewing compliance with a school's safety plan. This need has made your Later List because of some specific concern, but it's too complex an issue to solve using the Later List alone. The first step is to ask the correct person in the Accountability Circle, likely the operations director, to help the team determine the essence of the problem. In as concrete terms as possible, answer the question of what needs to be solved and where the process will be after ninety days. Of course, it's unlikely that an issue that has made Rock status will be completely solvable in that short a timeframe. But you need a smart, quarterly goal of specific, measurable, attainable, realistic actions to keep you moving forward. This goal becomes your Rock. A ninety-day goal in this instance might be to implement a new security system. This is beyond a normal Later List item that can be done in a week. It may include milestones such as researching vendors to upgrade door and window locking systems, getting bids from on-site security companies, making vendor selections, and scheduling installation.

It's important to note that as you move closer to the center of the Accountability Circle, you will encounter Sub-Rocks as well. The security plan may begin with the larger circle of district administration or even the school board, but it connects to site administrators, teachers, support staff, and even students. The board might earmark funding, the superintendent might choose the surveillance software, but teachers and students must be trained to lock the doors when a threat is detected.

When the big Rock is owned at the district level, it will facilitate the smooth handing off of Sub-Rocks to principals and other on-site staff. If this is done well, all the Rocks are coordinated to a larger purpose and set up to last.

Common Rocks Examples

Area	Rock Example
Instruction	Launch Tier 2 reading intervention pilot
HR	Cut average teacher hiring cycle from six weeks to four
Operations	Develop and approve updated school safety plan
Finance	Build three-year forecasting model for staffing
Student Services	Reduce chronic absenteeism from 6 to 3 percent
Leadership	Finalize and publish updated Vision document (chapter 15)

EXERCISE:

THE QUARTERLY PLANNING RHYTHM

In the FASCO system, every ninety days, your leadership team steps back to reflect and reset. This isn't a regular meeting. It's a quarter turn of the wheel—a deliberate pause to review, refocus, and re-align. The distraction-free, off-site setting is maximized to help evaluate which initiatives will receive your focus over the coming three months. Let's take a look at how you might set up this key event.

Frequency: Every ninety days

Duration: At least a half-day—ideally a full day; offsite if possible

Facilitator: Superintendent, cabinet leader, or external FASCO-trained coach

Welcome and Team Connection (15–30 min)
Open the session with an icebreaker or reflection round. Follow up with a team-building exercise or quick reconnect. Then, before discussion begins, reinforce the goal of the day: *Clarity, alignment, momentum.*

Look Back: The Last Ninety Days (30–60 min)
Without placing blame or allowing the conversation to wander into solutions, start the meeting with a quick review. Ask:

- What did we accomplish?
- What didn't get done and why? (maintain judgment-free posture)

- What needs to roll forward?
- Are we celebrating progress?

Then lead an abbreviated review of the past quarter's Rocks: those that were completed and those awaiting completion. What key things did your team learn during this process? What are they most proud of?

Vitals Review and Patterns (30 min)

- Are our core metrics healthy?
- What trends have emerged?
- What needs deeper attention or a new Rock?

Later List Scan (30–45 min)
Use your full Later List to determine what is mission-critical and timely. What should become a Rock this quarter (if anything)? What needs to stay parked?

Prioritize each item using the two questions from the Urgent + Important filter:

1. Is it urgent? Does this need to be solved this quarter?
   - Yes = time-sensitive, blocking progress, or has a deadline
   - No = can wait without major consequence
2. Is it important? Is this a mission-critical issue?
   - Yes = directly affects student outcomes, staff well-being, or strategic goals
   - No = helpful or interesting, but not essential

Set the Rocks (60–90 min)
These are your must-move priorities for the next ninety days, and they come with some guidelines for them to work efficiently.

Rules:

- Each person can own one or two Rocks at the most.
- The team collectively should have three to seven total Rocks.
- Each Rock must be clear, time-bound, and measurable, supporting your meeting goals of clarity, alignment, and momentum.

Use this format to record your results:

Rock Name—owned by [One Person]

Success looks like: [measurable outcome by ninety days]

Who Owns What? (15–30 min)

This is a key component to the process: Each Rock must be assigned to one person, just like the process of Vitals accountability. If multiple people express interest, encourage teamwork, but define who owns the Rock. Clarify expectations for weekly updates in huddles, and set deadlines or milestones if needed.

Team Exercise or Strategic Topic (Optional)

If time allows, take the opportunity for more in-depth discussion and collaboration in the following ways:

- Cross-functional working session
- Role clarity recalibration
- Revisiting core values or structure
- Guest speaker or district walk-through

Wrap-Up and Commitments (15 min)

As you conclude the meeting, finalize and share the Rock list and any tweaks to roles, core values, or structure. Confirm Rocks action steps with each responsible party, and set the next quarterly planning date.

End with sharing one-word answers to the following: "How are you leaving this meeting today?"

CONCLUSION

Rocks, in conjunction with the Later List and Vitals, all work together to manage your organization's energy. Rocks drive focused progress, the Later List protects that focus while keeping innovation alive, and Vitals continuously monitors the health of your entire system. When all those structures are in place, it's time to move to the most exciting phase of the FASCO process. It's time to explore your vision.

THE VISION: A BOLD MOVE

President Franklin D. Roosevelt said, "When the system is steady, the vision can be bold." Is your system ready for a bold Vision? Are you ready to paint a picture of where you are headed? If you have diligently established the foundation of the FASCO system, you can confidently answer, "Yes."

Many new FASCO users question why the Vision component comes after so many other core tools have already been put in place. Conventional wisdom says you must have a Vision before anything else, but the FASCO system is anything but conventional.

Let's consider the traditional mode of Vision creation. Most districts begin with a vision statement, strategic plan, or something like a *Portrait of a Graduate* to help set their long-term direction. Certainly, thinking through desired life skills and competencies for the students you serve has its place. Every district wants to graduate young adults who are global thinkers, collaborators, problem-solvers, and effective communicators. Every teacher dreams of pouring hours, days, and years into students' lives to see them become resilient, empathetic, productive members of their communities.

While dreaming of student success may sound like the logical first step, in a Fully Aligned Student-Centered Organization, we take a different path. Here's why: You can't draw a map without first gathering the tools to do so.

By establishing the Accountability Circle, Vitals, Later List, Rocks and Weekly Huddles, your team has the structure, language, and rhythm to actually implement a vision—not just talk about it.

In FASCO, Vision isn't an abstract document. It's a living tool that guides real decisions and drives the day-to-day work of the entire organization.

ARE YOU READY?

In many cases, the Vision component is a second-year initiative of the FASCO system. Effective change takes time, and you don't want to shortchange your team by forcing too much, too soon. You'll know your team is ready when:

- Weekly Huddles are happening consistently
- Each role owns clear Vitals
- At least one full quarter has been completed with Rocks
- Your leadership team is showing signs of shared ownership and trust

When all those pieces are in place, you are best set to rally your people and culture into seeing a clear picture of the organization as it moves into the future. What does your district stand for? What makes your school different from the one down the road? What would it look like if every one of the multitude of systems you are responsible for were aligned?

This is not a problem-solving exercise; it's a wide-open creative process. But in addition to being the perfect opportunity for the right-brain thinker to shine, creating a balanced vision will also incorporate pieces of logic and detail. Pieces that come from those who may not see themselves as creative. All team members have a place at the Vision table.

And although your team is firmly entrenched in the Accountability Circle model—the student is the center of all efforts—the Vision goes beyond the students. An effective Vision ripples into the teachers' lounge, the corner café, and the conference room where the school board meets every other Tuesday.

Of course, your district may already have a vigorous Vision statement in place. If that's the case, pull it out and revisit it. Especially if it is more than five years old, it may need some serious updating. If you are satisfied with it, reaffirm it and examine ways to better align your initiatives with its key points. Now that you have the FASCO tools in place, sharing your Vision will be second nature.

EXERCISE:
THE VISION RETREAT

Creating a powerful, shared Vision takes space—not just space on the calendar, but mental space.

We recommend a two-day off-site retreat, typically in the summer, to pause, zoom out, and create clarity for the coming three to five years. This should take place away from campus and distractions. Somewhere that encourages deep focus, conversation, and creativity.

Who Attends:

- Superintendent
- Cabinet/District Leaders
- Principals
- Key Facilitators (e.g., FASCO Coach if available)

A trained FASCO Coach brings neutral facilitation, proven process design, outside perspective, and the ability to challenge and stretch the team. Coaches are not required for your event to be a success, but they're often the difference between a good retreat and a transformational one.

Sample Two-Day Vision Retreat Agenda

Day 1: Reconnect + Reflect + Reframe

Time	Session
9:00–9:30	Welcome and Intentions for the Retreat
9:30–11:00	Team Reconnect Activity (values, motivations, mission grounding)
11:00–12:30	Review the Current State: Vitals, Rocks, Patterns
12:30–1:30	Lunch (offsite or catered)
1:30–3:00	What Does Success Look Like? Group Visioning Exercise
3:00–4:00	Build a Draft Vision (students, staff, system)
4:00–4:30	Reflections and Prep for Day 2

Day 2: Clarify + Align + Commit

Time	Session
9:00–9:30	Re-ground and Day 1 Recap
9:30–11:00	Finalize Vision Statements (Student Outcomes, Organizational Culture, System Design)
11:00–12:30	Align to Core Values + Accountability Circle
12:30–1:30	Lunch
1:30–3:00	What Must Be True? (Backwards Plan for Implementation)
3:00–4:00	Commitment Round: What Will I Do Differently Starting Now?
4:00–4:30	Close and Next Steps (Rocks, Communication Plan, Timeline)

Make a note of any unfinished discussions that began but were unrelated to the Vision process. Plan to follow up with team members about any private concerns or ideas.

READY TO CREATE YOUR VISION?

If your team has completed at least one full quarter using the FASCO tools—and Weekly Huddles, Vitals, the Later List, and Rocks are fully in place—then you're ready to lead a transformational conversation about the future.

This is your opportunity to define what student success truly looks like. It answers questions about what kind of organization you're building to support that goal. It provides a map to the path of alignment for every layer of the Accountability Circle.

The FASCO Alignment Hub features bespoke downloadable resources to help you plan and lead your Vision Retreat with clarity and purpose. This includes:

- Full facilitator agenda
- Group exercises and discussion prompts
- Sample vision statements
- Planning templates and follow-up tools

To access these tools and tap into the community of like-minded school leaders, visit www.ed-leaders.org/alignment-hub. There you will be able to download the complete Vision Toolkit and connect with others using FASCO. You may also inquire about pairing with a certified FASCO Coach, which is optional but highly recommended.

CONCLUSION

Creating a vision is one of the most satisfying processes any leader can facilitate. When you and your core team gather around unifying ideas and goals, your district or school will set itself apart from the average public service organization.

You don't have to figure it all out alone. FASCO is a system—and a community. We encourage you to log in to our website and explore all there is to learn from the years of expertise we've leaned into as FASCO continues to grow.

One of the crown jewels of the FASCO website is our documentation services. Through FASCO's Methods component, your organization has access to a variety of documentation tools that serve to bring consistent longevity to your processes. FASCO Methods ensure the results of your hard work will be there long after you have moved on.

METHODS: DOCUMENT WHAT WORKS

Some things happen predictably in school systems without fail every year: new hire training, parent-teacher conferences, kindergarten roundup, Friday night football, art fairs, graduation. These familiar processes and events bring comfort and nurture deep roots of tradition.

But what happens to kindergarten roundup the first fall after the teacher who coordinated things for the past two decades retires? How much chaos surrounds the book fair when the parent who volunteered to manage staffing and inventory suddenly ends up in the hospital? There doesn't have to be chaos if FASCO Methods are securely in place. Methods, or systematic documentation of procedures and processes, not only save us from the unexpected absence of our resident experts but also alleviate stress throughout the Accountability Circle.

WHY METHODS MATTER

You've done the work to build the right systems from Weekly Huddles to Vision Retreats. But unless those systems are clearly documented and consistently trained, they'll eventually devolve due to a number of issues. They may fall apart when someone leaves your organization. They may be reinterpreted or diluted as years pass. Oftentimes, they depend too heavily on individuals' strengths and get thrown out under new leadership. Like so many of the issues FASCO addresses, this is not a people problem; it's a system problem. And, as Alicia learned, system problems can be solved.

Strong Methods make your systems last beyond the people who created them. Methods create a legacy that will last for years to come.

WHAT MAKES A GOOD METHOD?

A Method is simply a documented, repeatable way of doing something that matters—something essential to the daily or quarterly rhythm of your Fully Aligned Student-Centered Organization.

A strong Method is the following:

- Clear: Anyone can follow it with minimal guidance
- Concise: Not a binder, not a free-for-all, just the essential steps
- Connected: Tied to your Accountability Circle, Vitals, or Rocks
- Trainable: Can be passed on easily and reinforced regularly

When deciding on which Methods to keep and which to discard, ask your team this question: Is this Method necessary and aligned with our Vision? You will find your systems becoming even more streamlined as you eliminate pointless recordkeeping.

Examples of What to Document as a Method

Area	Method Example
Weekly Huddles	Agenda, who facilitates, how Vitals and Later List are reviewed
Hiring	Interview flow, evaluation rubric, ACE Fit questions
Onboarding	First thirty-day checklist for new staff
Instruction	How we run PLCs or instructional coaching cycles
Operations	How to handle urgent facilities requests
Communication	Weekly staff update template and rhythm
Quarterly Planning	How we review Rocks, Vitals, and the Later List

Start with what's already working. If something is done well more than once, document it right away. Ask the transportation coordinator to share their Methods for pivoting in case of bad weather. Contact the food service director and get a copy of their to-do list for big events. Be sure to have written directions from anyone who coordinates a game at your school or in your district.

Like your Vision, your Methods are living documents. It's not enough to write out your processes and stick them in a file. They must be the following:

- Trained during onboarding
- Reviewed during quarterly planning
- Updated as new insights emerge

Assign someone to own each method—just like a Vital or a Rock. If it's important enough to standardize, it's important enough to maintain.

We recommend starting with FASCO's simple, digital tools to store and share your Methods. These education-centric tools can grow with you, leaving an organized, repeatable trail for those who follow.

The FASCO Alignment Hub keeps everything in one spot. You can run meetings, maintain your Later List, track your Vitals, and view the Accountability Circle all in one place. This online resource includes quizzes, videos, and workflows.

Ultimately, our vision is for all FASCO tools—including your documented Methods—to live inside the FASCO platform, seamlessly integrated with your Accountability Circle, Vitals, and Rocks.

CONCLUSION

You know what works: Sustainable systems provide scalable success. This is what every leader wants for their organization. Now that you have done what may have seemed impossible a few months or years ago—created enough margin for you and your team to do your jobs well—it's time to ensure the results of those efforts will remain for years to come. Establishing a strong foundation of FASCO Methods will create an environment where successes are repeatable and disappointments are documented. It's the final piece of the FASCO puzzle. And once that is in place, you can experience the clarity of a Fully Aligned Student-Centered Organization at its best.

EPILOGUE: QUICK-START GUIDE

If you're ready to start transforming your district into a Fully Aligned Student-Centered Organization, follow this simple path to implementation:

STEP 1: TAKE THE FASCO ASSESSMENT

See where your organization scores on alignment at www. ed-leaders.org/alignment-hub. This will serve as a starting point for you to assess your distinct needs. Some benefit from a full FASCO transformation; others may simply choose to use ideas in this book to improve existing modes of operation.

STEP 2: GIVE THIS BOOK TO YOUR LEADERSHIP TEAM

The first step to success with FASCO is to begin building a shared understanding among your leadership team. Distribute this book to principals, directors, and key district leaders, and ask them to read through the core tools. The biggest shift happens when everyone is on the same page and speaking the same language.

STEP 3: INTRODUCE THE ACCOUNTABILITY CIRCLE

At your next leadership meeting, redraw the way your district sees itself by introducing the Accountability Circle. Instead of the traditional top-down hierarchy, start framing your district's structure with students at the center, supported by teachers, site staff, district staff, and the school board.

Questions to discuss with your team:

✓ How do the FASCO principles change the way we think about leadership and responsibility?
✓ What do we need to do to grow and support each layer of the circle?
✓ How do we ensure that decisions align with this model?

STEP 4: ESTABLISH YOUR LEADERSHIP TEAM'S VITALS

Pick three to five key metrics that define the success and health of your district. These will guide every leadership meeting and serve as a real-time dashboard of what matters most.

Example Vitals:

✓ Third-Grade Reading Proficiency: This is a strong indicator of long-term success.
✓ Student Attendance Rates: If kids aren't in school, they're not learning.
✓ Teacher Retention: If staff are leaving, something is broken.
✓ Budget Alignment: Ensuring financial health for long-term stability.

Once you establish your Vitals, start every leadership meeting by reviewing them. If a Vital is slipping, it becomes the top priority before any new initiatives are introduced.

STEP 5: INTRODUCE THE LATER LIST

Start using the Later List in leadership meetings to track important but not urgent issues. This will prevent your team from feeling overwhelmed and allow you to proactively tackle challenges at the right time.

How to Use the Later List:

- ✓ Create a shared document where team members can add items that need attention.
- ✓ Review the list weekly, ranking items by importance and urgency.
- ✓ Move key items into action when the time is right.

This tool alone will dramatically improve focus by helping your team prioritize. It will also help you avoid reactionary leadership.

By taking these four steps, you will immediately start aligning your leadership team and setting the foundation for a sustainable, student-centered district.

Remember: implementing FASCO—all or part of the system—does not add more to your plate; it creates clarity regarding what's already sitting there.

Start today. One step at a time.

Visit www.ed-leaders.org to download the tools and connect with other education leaders on this journey.

SOURCES

Traction, Gino Wickman

Get a Grip, Gino Wickman and Mike Paton

The Gap and the Gain, Dan Sullivan with Dr. Benjamin Hardy

Who Not How, Dan Sullivan with Dr. Benjamin Hardy

The 4 Disciplines of Execution, Chris McChesney, Sean Covey, and Jim Huling

Start with Why, Simon Sinek

The Five Dysfunctions of a Team, Patrick Lencioni

Five Obsessions of Elite Organizations, Michael Erath

The ONE Thing, Gary Keller with Jay Papasan

Process!, Mike Paton with Lisa Gonzalez

The 6 Types of Working Genius, Patrick Lencioni

The Energy Bus, Jon Gordon

Rocket Fuel, Gino Wickman and Mark C. Winters

Hero on a Mission, Donald Miller

Ego Is the Enemy, Ryan Holiday

The 16 Undeniable Laws of Communication, John Maxwell

Crucial Conversations, Joseph Grenny, Kerry Patterson, Ron McMillan, Al Switzler, and Emily Gregory

The Advantage, Patrick Lencioni

The Self-Driven Child, William Stixrud, PhD, and Ned Johnson

The 7 Habits of Highly Effective People, Stephen R. Covey

Drive, Daniel H. Pink

The Infinite Game, Simon Sinek

Leadership and Self-Deception, The Arbinger Institute

Impact Players, Liz Wiseman

Essentialism, Greg McKeown

Extreme Ownership, Jocko Willink and Leif Babin

Love Does, Bob Goff

Mindset, Carol Dweck

Atomic Habits, James Clear

The Coaching Habit, Michael Bungay Stanier

Good to Great, Jim Collins

The Obstacle Is the Way, Ryan Holiday

Grit, Angela Duckworth

The End of Average, Todd Rose

What Got You Here Won't Get You There, Marshall Goldsmith

ACKNOWLEDGMENTS

First, to my wife, Darci—thank you for being the steady, thoughtful presence beside me on every Saturday morning hike. You've listened to countless half-formed ideas, challenged the ones that needed sharpening, and offered insights that made this book better than it ever could have been on my own. Your support is the quiet engine behind so much of this work.

To my kids—Grant, Maggie, and Tessa. Seeing the world through your eyes reminds me why this work matters. Your curiosity, your humor, and the way each of you navigates school in your own way keep me motivated to push for environments where every student can thrive. You are the daily reminder of the stakes.

To the board of ELO—Ellen Perconti, Cory Steiner, Brad Uchacz, Joe Fisher, and Tim Powers. Thank you for being a sounding board, a challenge function, and a well of real-world wisdom. Your lived experience as school leaders helped shape the ideas in these pages, grounding them in the realities of the work.

To Mike Duncan—for years, I searched for a superintendent who had implemented a system like this into their district. Not only did you have the practical experience, but also your conversations and insights added clarity throughout the development of FASCO as a true thought partner.

To Traci Matt and the entire Streamline team—thank you for guiding this project with patience, persistence, and a belief in what it can mean for education. You kept the momentum going even when my attention wandered elsewhere, always bringing me back to the bigger impact.

To Jill Simonds—your ability to turn ideas into action is a gift. Thank you for leading the charge, organizing the chaos, and bringing clarity to the process. You've been the true integrator who helped make this book a reality.

To Entrepreneurs' Organization, and all my current and past forum mates—so many of the concepts within FASCO were shaped by the lessons, failures, breakthroughs, and honest conversations we've shared. You taught me that "good enough" is never enough when the mission matters, and that perspective lives on in these pages.

Finally, to everyone who has contributed ideas, feedback, encouragement, or a gentle nudge along the way—thank you. This book is the product of collective wisdom and shared purpose, inspired by the people who tirelessly work to improve education for every student.

ABOUT THE AUTHOR

Kevin Stoller believes that if we truly want to improve education, we must start by supporting the people leading our schools. As executive director of the Education Leaders' Organization (ELO), he is dedicated to helping school leaders align their teams and communities around what matters most—students. His mission is simple yet urgent: to give every student the best opportunity to succeed by equipping school leaders with the clarity, structure, and support they deserve.

When he's not working with school leaders, Kevin's favorite role is with his family. After growing up in the Midwest, Kevin, his wife, Darci, and their three kids made the move to Arizona, where snow days turned into sunshine, hikes, and the goal to find every body of water within driving distance. Kevin still carries his Midwestern roots with him—grounded, family-focused, and fueled by a belief that the right people, when aligned around the right mission, can change lives for generations to come.